Praise for *Trend-Driven Innovation*

"If you're an innovator, designer, entrepreneur or in need of one, read this book. It is entertaining and pathologically precise, and unveils a simple and elegant system for spotting early trends that may reshape our business, community and life."

Lisa Gansky

— Entrepreneur; Author of *The Mesh*

"This book is a highly contemporary insight into how the world is changing that goes beyond the obvious and anticipated. Leaders who are focused on delivering what people will want should pay these insights great attention now."

David Bartlett

— Chairman, Future Industries Fund Advisory Council; Former Premier of Tasmania

"Some of the smartest thinking about the swiftest way to get the answers to what drives consumers in the hypercompetitive, hyperconnected era where the customer isn't just always right, they are ahead of the commercial producer almost every time."

Julia Hobsbawm

— Founder, Editorial Intelligence; Honorary Visiting Professor in Networking, Cass Business School, London

"As an entrepreneur, you intuitively 'get' the trend you're riding. But as you scale you need to understand how to deal with the next wave of trends too. Trend-Driven Innovation is a practical guide that we're using to do just that."

Cassandra Stavrou

— Founder, Propercorn

TREND-DRIVEN INNOVATION

Beat accelerating customer expectations with

TREND DRIVEN INNOVATION

Henry Mason, David Mattin, Maxwell Luthy, Delia Dumitrescu
Designed by Maria Isabel Reyes

WILEY

[CONTENTS]

1 WHY NOW

2 SCAN

3 FOCUS

Welcome to the Expectation Economy

The Overwhelm Is the Opportunity

What to Run With, When, and How

EXECUTE

Turn Insights into Ideas

Realize Your Ideas,
or Realize They Are Useless

Unlock an Opportunity
Machine

Alexander Osterwalder

Cofounder of Strategyzer and lead author of *Business Model Generation* and *Value Proposition Design*.

Every business hopes to be successful. But it's the ability to navigate and understand trends that separates the successful companies from the crowded field of "innovators." If you don't have the ability to understand trends and their implications to your business, you run the risk of becoming irrelevant.

A smart business understands how to identify trends that may reshape its future. A smart business picks trends that allow it to experiment with new business models and value propositions—their testing, adaptation, and implementation, instead of spending money and resources on the one "right idea."

In 2004, I published *Business Model Generation*, and the accompanying *Business Model Canvas*, to provide businesses with a framework for innovation. My company Strategyzer expands on this mission and provides software that encourages constant experimentation, failure, and iteration. The canvas is used by millions of people, and we've convinced large corporations like 3M, Mastercard, Colgate, GE, and Nestlé to take advantage of the techniques that so many people have found to be successful.

The challenge is to use trends to advance business models (the foundation that keeps a company alive and able to create profit) while offering value propositions that attract customers and differentiate you from competitors. Both of these concepts run the risk of expiring like yogurt in the fridge if they are left to sit idle for far too long. We're seeing this happen to the corporations that built dominance in another era. The key is to build a portfolio of experiments that help minimize the risk of "getting it wrong." Some of your tests will fail, some will succeed, but overall you will find success if your business is focused on conducting a series of proactive experiments. The challenging part is to carry out all this exploration while executing, managing, and improving the existing business.

The team at TrendWatching provides content and tools that capture shifts in consumer behavior. They give businesses an important launchpad to shape ideas, develop new business models, and offer unique value propositions to customers. *Trend-Driven Innovation* is a straightforward yet comprehensive starting point to help businesses understand the shifts that will drive future business growth and success.

Trends aren't new to business development, but the businesses that understand how to identify and act on new consumer behaviors and market dynamics will have a leg up on innovation—creating value for their customers and driving profits—and will lead in their industries.

How We Came to Write This Book

This book makes a bold claim: to get you ahead of customers' accelerating expectations. What makes us think we can promise that? And why—with 22,435 books added to Amazon's Business & Money category *in the last 90 days alone*—should you trust us to deliver?

A lot has changed since 2002 when we started writing about trends and innovation. It's hard to remember, but back then, swipes and taps weren't anything other than physical gestures. You hailed taxis with a wave. Mark Zuckerberg was in high school. The BRICs had just been named. Buy One Give One and the Collaborative Economy weren't known business models. Indeed, when we started watching trends, neither crowdsourcing nor freemium—the two central innovations of *our* business model—had even been coined as terms yet! Trends were something that gurus revealed in expensive and closely guarded reports and presentations.

We turned that model on its head. We gave away Trend Briefings for free online. We invited our most passionate readers to join our global trend spotting network. It worked: over the past 13 years, we've grown from three people in a canal house in Amsterdam to teams in London, New York, São Paulo, Singapore, and Lagos, all supported by nearly 3,000 trend spotters in over 100 countries. Professionals at 96 percent of Interbrand's Best Global Brands read our trend insights. Our online trend platform is currently used by over 1,200 brands, agencies, consultancies, nonprofits, and schools. We do more than 50 in-person trend sessions and workshops a year. And we still send free trends to over a quarter of a million subscribers every month.

But clients, spotters, and audiences constantly challenge us as we do all this. Where did that trend come from? Will it last? Where's it headed? What does it mean? Does it matter? What can I do with it?

This book explains how we answer those questions. Rather than offer you a compilation of what's hot today—that will end up in tomorrow's bargain bin—these pages contain our complete, end-to-end trend methodology. Crucially, they enable you to answer perhaps the most important question of all: how will *you* successfully and repeatedly spot, track, prioritize, act on, deploy, and get ahead of trends?

You will look at the world differently after reading this book. You will be able to anticipate what your customers will want next. You—and your organization—will be more successful. But beyond financial success, trend-driven innovation also promises more than that. Ultimately, everyone wants a better future: for themselves, society, and the planet. We can create that better future. Indeed, we have a responsibility to do so. Let's not shy away from it; let's enjoy it.

—**Henry, David, Max, Delia**
April 2015

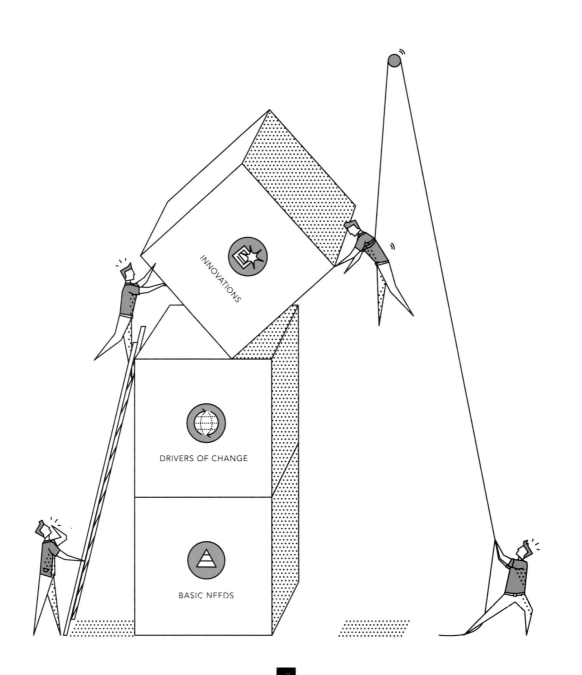

INNOVATIONS

DRIVERS OF CHANGE

BASIC NEEDS

To access supporting material, practice exercises, interactive versions of the featured tools, templates, and more, head to:

TREND DRIVEN INNOVATION .COM

This bonus content is exclusively available to people who own this book, so you'll need your copy on hand to register for access.

WHY NOW

WELCOME TO THE EXPECTATION ECONOMY

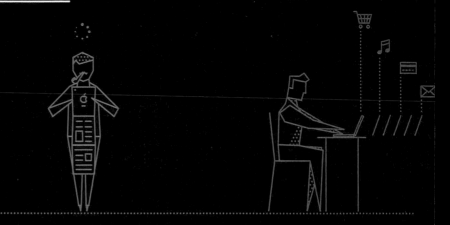

You're reading this because you want to create organizations, products, services, or campaigns that delight people. But the very people you're targeting are raising their expectations at an ever-accelerating rate, making them seemingly impossible to even satisfy— let alone delight.

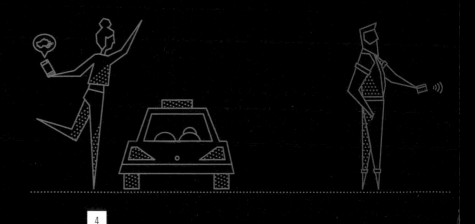

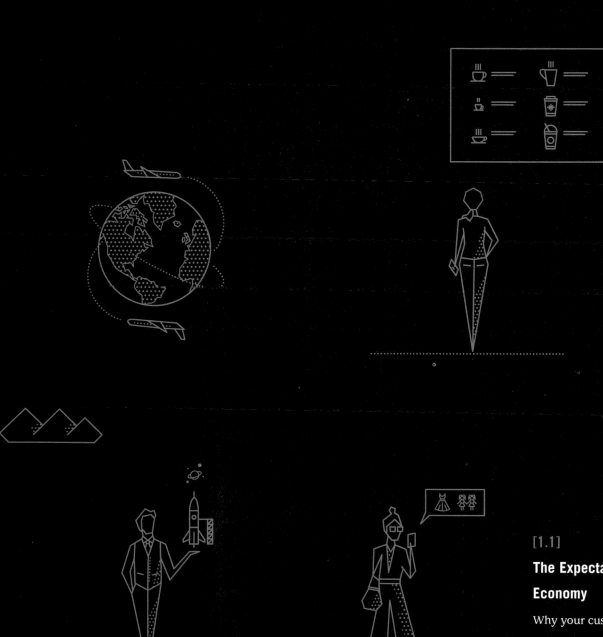

[1.1]

The Expectation Economy

Why your customers are (almost) impossible to please.

THE EXPECTATION ECONOMY

Why your customers are (almost) impossible to please.

A GLOBAL SNAPSHOT

In Manila, a mother pulls out her Chinese-designed Xiaomi smartphone, opens the GrabTaxi app and hails a cab, while her son uses his phone to track her arrival turn-by-turn. In Brazil, 450 tattoo artists warn clients of high-risk moles after being trained on how to spot signs of skin cancer by suncare brand Sol de Janeiro. In downtown Manhattan, a shopper stops on West 22nd Street to purchase a $200 pair of earphones that have been custom-printed to fit perfectly into her ears.

The remarkable aspect of all this is how unremarkable it has become.

Look past the clichés about how "business as usual is over" and on "the relentless pace of change" and you'll see the great paradox in today's business arena: the truly exceptional has become wholly unexceptional.

Customers—them, you, me, all of us—are no longer marveling at how efficiently global markets satisfy our mindboggling array of needs and wants. Instead, we merely rage at any moment of failure.

And despite the global consumer arena being more diverse and varied than it has ever been, its inhabitants share a common mind-set: astonishingly elevated expectations, set at the high watermark not of personal but of collective experience, and applied ruthlessly to each and every business, product, service, or experience available.

Welcome to the Expectation Economy.

THREE STRANDS OF EXPECTATION

THE EXPECTATION ECONOMY: AN ECONOMY OF EVER-ACCELERATING CUSTOMER EXPECTATIONS, APPLIED RUTHLESSLY TO EVERY PURCHASE DECISION, EXPERIENCE, AND MOMENT OF ATTENTION.

The Expectation Economy is built on the convergence of three strands of customer expectation: rising quality, positive impact, and personal expression. These give customers significant power and control, while businesses are left chasing—and never quite catching up with—the curve of accelerating expectations.

But if you understand where and how these expectations are growing, you can start to change that. Let's get going.

[1] **RISING QUALITY**

Near-total transparency now sees organizations that deliver anything less than the best die an increasingly rapid death. Meanwhile, the ability and pace at which new entrants can find their way into the hands of customers continues to accelerate. Taken together, these changes ensure that customer expectation of new products and services is (rightly) cycling higher and higher.

[2] **POSITIVE IMPACT**

Rising and unavoidable awareness of the impact of their actions is leaving many people trapped in a guilt spiral over the negative environmental, social, and health impacts of their consumption. Combine this with the growing number of ethical and sustainable (often startup) businesses, and the result is an expectation that new products and services will offer continued indulgence, but without the guilt.

[3] **PERSONAL EXPRESSION**

In today's societies of material abundance, customers are increasingly prioritizing self-improvement and personal expression. Diverse forms of status currency—knowledge, taste, reach, and more—are combining with changes in the way people value new experiences and connect to one another, to offer consumers new avenues of personal expression through consumption. The result? Customers expect not only to have more, but to *be* more.

[1] RISING QUALITY

Why today's best is never quite good enough.

No one who serves customers today is remotely surprised by the contention that they demand the highest quality and service.

But it's the expectation of *rising* quality that explains why today's customers are never satisfied with what they have—or even the best on offer—and will instead continue to seek newer, faster, more affordable, more exciting, simply "better" options.

To understand this race to the top—and to prosper inside it—it pays to appreciate the forces driving customer expectations of quality:

- **Transparency Triumph** and the survival of the best.
- **Creative Destruction** and the many benefits it brings people.
- **Easy Experimentation** and a tendency toward greater access to—and trust of—the new.

TRANSPARENCY TRIUMPH

The last two decades have seen the web drive a revolution in transparency that has transformed many aspects of the consumer and business arena. Yadda yadda . . . so far, so 1999.

However, the real and, dare we say, interesting implication of TRANSPARENCY TRIUMPH is that finally, the survival rate for businesses that fail to delight customers is approaching zero.

This is because near-perfect and near-instant information has pushed the uninformed customer—one unable to locate the best possible option—close to extinction. Armed with a smartphone, no matter where customers are or what they are seeking, the views and experiences of others—and with them, the security of pre-purchase confidence—are but a tap away.

Of course, in a world where even certain models of paper shredder have over 4,000 reviews on Amazon, customers now know just as well as business professionals that it's getting tougher for the second best (let alone third, fourth, and beyond) to survive, too. The result? Ever-intensifying expectations of high-quality products, services, and experiences, and the valid expectation that future standards will be even higher as all but the best are driven out.

DOMINO'S PIZZA

The turnaround of U.S. pizza chain Domino's between 2009 and 2014 is a compelling case study in how transparency can (nearly) kill an underperforming business. And how a deep understanding of how to harness transparency can save it.

In 2009, Domino's pizza sales were in massive decline, as customers responded to poor reviews and deserted it for rivals Pizza Hut and Papa John's, whom they perceived as better value and higher quality, respectively. When employees uploaded a video to YouTube that showed them violating the food they were preparing, the company reached its nadir.

In response, the pizza chain acknowledged and embraced the near-perfect information available to consumers. It acknowledged customer reviews that called

out their "boring, bland, mass-produced pizza." In December 2009 it launched *The Pizza Turnaround*, a documentary detailing how the chain had "reinvented its pizza from the crust up." Domino's invited customers to post photos of its food on the brand's site and published them unadulterated. The campaign continued with initiatives including customer feedback broadcast in Times Square and a live video stream placed in a Salt Lake City restaurant kitchen. Sales rebounded, and between 2009 and 2014 the chain opened 1,800 new stores in 10 countries.

Companies don't spend millions showing you their product in its worst form . . . [but] we're honest and open with our issues. We'll address them head-on.

Patrick Doyle, CEO, Domino's Pizza

CREATIVE DESTRUCTION

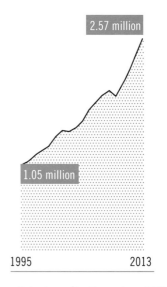

Patent applications since 1995

The words "creative destruction" send a chill up the spine of countless business executives. After all, it's the force that threatens to sweep you out of the market and into irrelevance, right?

Customers, however, see the current wave of creative destruction as something to be celebrated. That's because it brings an endless stream of new products and services, each better than the last.

Today, new innovations are emerging hourly, from all corners of the globe. These innovations are fueled by the incredible democratization and globalization of innovation and manufacturing tools, from crowdfunding to 3D printing to app stores and more. This revolution has put immense creative power in the hands of people around the world, ensured that the best can come from anywhere, and radically transformed perceptions about who can be an innovator.

Of course, it doesn't necessarily hold that more innovation equals better innovation. But transparent markets that are filled with a greater volume of new ideas, more new entrants, and more efficient matching of needs with innovations (see overleaf) inevitably become a more hostile environment to old, tired, and lower-quality offerings.

The result? An upward cycle in product and service quality, and in customer expectations of quality.

Willingness to wait in a city, 2013 vs. 2014

[FEATURE]

UBER: HOW NEWCOMERS TRANSFORM EXPECTATION

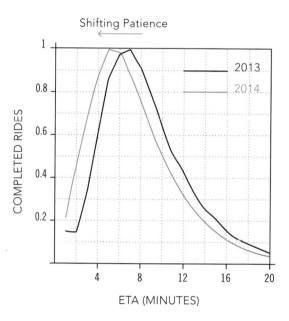

Consumer expectation can sometimes seem an intangible substance: hard to see, even harder to quantify. And that can make it difficult to perceive the impact of new, higher-quality entrants on expectation.

In January 2015, transportation provider Uber made public a dataset that provides a remarkable glimpse of the Expectation Economy in action.

Uber's data looked at how the estimated driver arrival time shown to users influenced their decision to complete or cancel a planned trip. In city after city the pattern was clear: the longer Uber had been operating in the city, the less patient users became when it came to pickup times (as shown above). In short, as the inhabitants of a city became more familiar with Uber, their expectations of fast pickup increased. The implication, in Uber's own words? "We realize we have to continually raise the bar."

We couldn't have put it better ourselves.

EASY EXPERIMENTATION

So, your customers harbor expectations of rising quality. But those same customers are also more able—and more prone—than ever to experiment: enthusiastically diving into a never-ending stream of new products, services, and experiences in their search for the best available option. Why?

First, trying new products and services is less risky than ever. The new Samsung smartphone? See it unboxed and discussed on YouTube before buying. A subscription to a new makeup curation and delivery service? Read nine reviews on a trusted beauty forum before signing up.

Second, virtual products and services encourage experimentation. From yet another mobile photo app downloaded and discarded, to another Kindle e-book sample hastily skimmed, digital products are low risk and low cost (if they cost anything at all), and so can be tried and discarded at will.

Third, subscription or rental business models (from Birchbox to Rent the Runway) allow people to experience physical products for less financial outlay, while online retailers will often not only pay for return shipping, they'll include a preprinted returns label!

Finally, all this experimentation becomes a self-accelerating cycle as more people try out new products and services and share their experience, creating a virtuous (for customers) and challenging (for innovators) circle of ever more experimentation, ever greater transparency, and ever higher expectation.

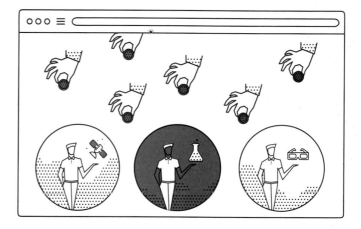

[FEATURE]
PRE-TAIL PLATFORMS: EDGING CLOSER TO PERFECT MARKET FIT

One further glimpse of the new innovation landscape: crowdfunding platforms such as Kickstarter or IndieGogo or Brazil's Catarse or China's DemoHour.

By allowing innovators to test the market for new ideas with almost zero risk, these sites act as catalysts for innovation. The ideas that prove popular secure funding, while others simply die a relatively inexpensive (if not zero cost) death.

Take the Pebble Smartwatch. Funded to the tune of $10.2 million in just 30 days in 2012, it helped establish the category that Google and Apple later entered (while by January 2015, Pebble had sold its millionth watch). Similarly, the potential of these platforms is shown by the Oculus Rift virtual reality headset, which raised $2.4 million in late 2012 before being bought by Facebook just 18 months later, for $2 *billion*.

It's not just gadgets being funded: *The Square* (a film about the Egyptian revolution) was nominated for an Oscar, while artist and activist Ai Weiwei funded his exhibition on Alcatraz Island via Kickstarter.

Indeed, the near zero-risk environment that crowdfunding offers innovators means that the diversity, inventiveness, and sheer number of innovations on offer are finally coming close to matching the diversity of people's needs, wants, and preferences.

In the years ahead, as more innovators turn to crowdfunding to test the market for their innovations and creative projects, they will further push up your customers' expectations of what is possible.

 # [2] POSITIVE IMPACT

A race to escape the guilt spiral.

We can see the second strand of the Expectation Economy at work as we look at the common threads that unite many of today's most talked-about brands—from Tesla to Patagonia, Chipotle to TOMS.

These expectation-setting brands embody the rising demand for products and experiences that customers can enjoy without feeling guilty at the impact they are wreaking on themselves, society, or the planet.

And alongside the relentless disruption that these challengers represent, we can detect a further expectation shift: when it comes to deciding whom to trust with delivering positive impact, customers are lavishing love and attention on new and barely proven startups far more enthusiastically than on established incumbents. In short, people expect all brands to be good, but they assume newer brands will be better.

Understand these two forces, and you'll be well-positioned to deliver the positive and meaningful impact that customers expect.

GUILT-FREE CONSUMPTION

Let's start with a truth all optimists hold self-evident: people are inherently "good" and, all things being equal, they want to have a positive impact on the world, or at least avoid having a negative impact.

However, pervasive transparency has made the negative impacts of much consumption—on the planet, other people, and oneself—ever harder to ignore.

The result? Rising numbers of people feel trapped in a guilt spiral over the negative impacts of their lifestyles and would like to change. But too often, a mixture of necessity, habit, and yes, lack of willpower means limited success. Cue more guilt.

It's ultimately this tension that sits at the heart of the sustainability mega-trend. Forget the science; what's more relevant to businesspeople is that millions are in search of— and increasingly expect—a new consumerism, one with reduced negative impact or, better yet, downright *positive* impact.

IN THE EXPECTATION ECONOMY, THE ULTIMATE LUXURY IS FREEDOM FROM THE GUILT SPIRAL.

[FEATURE]
TESLA

In little more than a decade, California-based Tesla Motors has become one of the iconic brands of the early twenty-first century. Of course, billionaire founder Elon Musk, great design, and burgeoning interest in innovative new automotive technologies have all helped. But Tesla's brand identity is about more than that.

Fundamentally, Tesla's hold over the customer consciousness reflects a new and powerful impulse toward a consumerism that allows continued indulgence while absolving guilt over negative environmental, social, and health impacts. At the heart of the Tesla brand is a mission to reconcile those two seemingly contradictory imperatives. The Tesla Model S does just that, providing all the indulgence and excitement of a traditional sports car—a sporty design, great performance, eye-catching look—while alleviating guilt by employing cutting-edge lithium-ion batteries to minimize environmental impact.

And it appears to be working: in October 2014, automotive intelligence firm JATO reported that in Europe in the preceding month the Tesla Model S outsold established rivals such as the BMW 7-Series and Audi A8.

[FEATURE]
PATAGONIA

During the past five years, U.S. outdoor clothes manufacturer Patagonia has taken repeated steps to further cement its reputation as a company that puts environmental and social purpose at the heart of everything it does.

In 2011, while other retailers were blasting their mailing lists with Black Friday promotions, Patagonia sent an email to its customers with the headline: "Do Not Buy This Jacket." The email then promoted the company's Common Threads eBay platform, where customers can buy and sell secondhand Patagonia clothing (Patagonia makes no money from the sales). In 2012, it launched The Footprint Chronicles, a platform allowing users to track the environmental impacts of its supply chain. The following year saw the launch of $20 Million & Change, its corporate venturing arm, investing in environmentally minded startups. Late in 2014, the company announced its Traceable Down initiative, allowing customers to trace any down used in Patagonia clothes back to birds that have not been force fed or live plucked.

For Patagonia's founder Yvon Chouinard, these initiatives are simply a natural extension of the company's mission statement, which is to "build the best product, cause no unnecessary harm, use business to inspire and implement solutions to the environmental crisis." And they appear to be working: in 2012, Patagonia revenue rose by a third year-on-year to $543 million, while in 2013 it rose a further 6 percent to $575 million.

CLEAN SLATE BRANDS

Traditional brand theory suggests that history and heritage are valuable assets that lie at the heart of a brand's ability to attract and retain customer attention. However, we're witnessing a profound shift in power in the business arena, one that calls this "truth" into question.

The new truth is that customers are now as attracted (if not more so) to unproven brands and organizations as they were to established ones in the past.

They expect the new—that means the startup, legacy-free, even unknown brand—to be more trustworthy, ethical, and simply better than established brands.

Indeed, as the hostility shown toward incumbents, from banks and fast food chains to big pharma demonstrates, "established" is now often just another word for unsustainable, unethical, unhealthy, unresponsive, untrusted, and most likely less compelling than more recent entrants.

Once you understand this counter-intuitive insight, customer attitudes to brands as diverse as Sustain (an ethical condom startup) to Venmo (a disruptive peer-to-peer payment service) to Lockitron (a mobile-controlled smartlock) start to make sense.

Lockitron is a device that allows users to lock, unlock, and share access to their front door remotely through their mobile. Initially rejected by Kickstarter, Lockitron formed its own crowdfunding campaign to raise funds to develop the device through preorders. Its initial goal of $150,000 was hit within 24 hours, and five days after launching, the company had raised $1.5 million! Ask yourself: would customers have trusted the security of their homes to an unproven startup a decade ago?

Yet the faith that customers are putting in newer, lesser-known brands is not unfounded. By dint of being more agile, and with easy access to innovation tools, startup brands *are* often better than their established counterparts. What's more, the fact that they are (by definition) newly established means the new business values that customers expect—

higher environmental, ethical, and social standards, and transparency—are often deeply embedded in their business models and practices from the start.

Contrast this with the empty corporate values which legacy brands espouse—remember BP's "Beyond Petroleum"—that then ring hollow in the face of exposé after exposé about worker exploitation, harmful processes, and mind-sets (no matter that these may have been established in a different era, under different expectations).

The rush to these CLEAN SLATE BRANDS has created a virtuous circle, in which new brands that offer higher quality and more ethical and sustainable practices raise consumer expectations (of continued indulgence minus guilt), while that expectation itself fuels the success of an even greater number of even newer CLEAN SLATE BRANDS.

[3] PERSONAL EXPRESSION

Me—only better.

Today, your customers don't just want—and expect—to have more (of ever higher quality). They don't just want to escape guilt (or even do good). They expect to *be* more, too.

Enter the third and final strand of the Expectation Economy: rising expectation among your customers that consumption will deliver personal advancement, meaning, and identity. In short, customers are looking for the organizations they spent time and money supporting, the products they use, and the experiences they have to help them be the people they want to be and to make real the idealized versions of themselves that they carry around in their head. Indeed, examine many of the brands that seem to best tap into the cultural and consumer zeitgeist—from Nike and Instagram to Khan Academy and Airbnb—and you'll find they do just that. Let's see how.

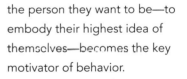

ABUNDANCE AND SELF-ACTUALIZATION

The Quantified Self movement. The explosion in online education and MOOCs (Massive Open Online Courses). Mindfulness. FOMO (Fear of Missing Out). An endless ocean of high-quality, creative, user-generated content. All are manifestations of the rising expectation that consumption will deliver personal improvement.

What's driving this? At heart, it's about the impact that abundance has on the way people think about themselves, and their relationship to the world.

It's likely that many—and in some cases all—of your customers live in societies of once undreamed of material abundance. Societies in which people have, by historical standards, an abundance of "stuff."

Does this mean the end of the story for consumerism? Hardly. As far back as 1943, psychologist Abraham Maslow identified "self-actualization" as the final, elusive imperative that drives human behavior once basic needs are met.

As material abundance becomes the norm, the drive to become

the person they want to be—to embody their highest idea of themselves—becomes the key motivator of behavior.

In today's affluent consumer societies, that drive means decision making on new products, services, and experiences becomes inextricably linked to identity. Through their consumption, your customers are pursuing nothing less than the self-improvement— physical, mental, emotional, spiritual—that can help them transform into their ideal selves.

NIKE

Nike has built an entire brand ethos—
and revenues of around $7 billion per
quarter—around the endless quest
for self-actualization. These examples
provide a glimpse of how they did it
in 2014.

FIND YOUR GREATNESS.

QUANTIFIED SELF AND GAMIFICATION

URBAN RUNNERS ENCOURAGED TO
REPRESENT NEIGHBORHOODS

Ahead of the We Run MX event
in Mexico City during November
2014, Nike created 11 different
clans to represent areas of the
city. Runners could join a team
and upload their training data via
the Nike+ service. A leaderboard
ranked the clans based on the
kilometers run, and participants
could unlock Nike+ awards for their
pre-race training.

REWARDING GOOD BEHAVIOR

VENDING MACHINE ACCEPTS
FUELBAND POINTS AS CURRENCY

July 2014 saw the installation of
special vending machines, called
Fuelboxes, across New York City.
The machines dispensed Nike
products only in exchange for
points accrued with the brand's
fitness wearable, the FuelBand,
within the last 24 hours. Users
plugged their devices into the
machine to pay for items such as
shirts, socks, and hats.

GUILT-FREE CONSUMPTION

ECO-FRIENDLY CONCEPT STORES
MADE FROM E-WASTE

Opened in cities including London,
New York, Shanghai, and Hong
Kong during June 2014, NikeLab
is a series of experimental concept
stores designed for maximum eco-
sustainability. Each one features
modular fixtures made out of
recycled electronic waste, with
structures held together without
the use of chemicals.

People now demand us not to say "Just do it"; they say, "Help me just do it." "Enable me to just do it." And the role of the brand changes from one of inspiration to one of inspiration and enablement.

Stephan Olander,
VP Digital Sport, Nike

STATUS DIVERSIFICATION

The pursuit of self-actualization is not just about *who I am*; it's about *who I am and am seen to be*. It's not enough for people to fulfill their potential. They want others to see it, too.

We all know what traditional consumer status looked like: the conspicuous consumption that declared "I am financially successful." But material abundance means that many of the old status symbols—cars, condos, credit cards—have lost much of their power. Instead, we're amid the rise of a post-material "statusphere" in which overt displays of financial success are accompanied and sometimes replaced by other, more diverse forms of status currencies, such as the three below:

[a] As people become immersed in the creative and knowledge economies, STATUS SKILLS— the acquisition and display of knowledge and expertise—become ever more prized.

[b] Abundant choice has also led people to strive to tell ever more interesting STATUS STORIES via products, materials, services, and experiences with compelling backstories that (often implicitly) speak volumes about the tastes and sensibilities of the user.

[c] The pervasiveness of a life lived publicly (or if not publicly, then at the very least, shared on social media with friends and family) has amplified digital status expression, making online status perhaps the most valuable personal social currency of all.

Just three shards of the Expectation Economy's fragmented statusphere:

STATUS SKILLS: FLOW HIVE

NO BEEKEEPING SUIT REQUIRED:
HOMEMADE HONEY ON TAP

Flow Hive is an artificial honeycomb system that enables hobbyist beekeepers to extract honey by simply turning a faucet (rather than having to smoke the bees out and remove the frames). It raised over $8 million from aspiring beekeepers during its crowdfunding campaign in early 2015.

STATUS STORIES: BRAHMA

BEER GROWN UNDER THE FEET OF
BRAZILIAN SOCCER STARS

To commemorate its sponsorship of the 2014 Soccer World Cup and the national team, Brazilian beer brand Brahma released Seleção Especial. The limited edition beer was made from barley that had been grown on the field where the Brazilian soccer team had trained.

ONLINE STATUS: W HOTELS

SOCIAL MEDIA SERVICE FOR
WEDDING COUPLES

In March 2014, New York City's four W Hotels began to offer a social media concierge service for weddings. For $3,000 guests can have their wedding showcased across social media with live hashtagged tweets and Instagram photos and videos. Niche now, common practice in the future?

EXPERIENCE CRAMMING

One important manifestation of the diversification in status is the long-lasting shift away from the acquisiton of products and toward the acquisition of experiences. Of course, that's nothing new. Way back in 1998, business thinkers Joseph Pine and James Gilmore coined a term for it: the Experience Economy. The searching out of new, rare, and status-worthy experiences—and the acquison of great memories—were the defining behaviors of Pine and Gilmore's Experience Economy.

Fast-forward almost 20 years, and we're now in the Expectation Economy (another "Economy"!). Here, experiences that few others can or have had remain a sure-fire status symbol, but due to the near-overwhelming number of experiences available and the sheer number of people in pursuit of unique experiences, truly exceptional experiences are becoming hard to find, and often out of reach for those without limitless budgets.

The cheaper, more practical alternative is to turn to EXPERIENCE CRAMMING: collecting and mixing and matching as many, and as wide a variety, of new experiences as possible to form a collage that uniquely reflects the individual (and how interesting they are).

And with a growing number of businesses, from low-cost airlines to energy-drink-cum-media-platforms to experience-rich, pop-up retailers catering to this behavior, customer expectation around experiences—and what they need to offer—continues to ramp ever higher.

[FEATURE]
SELFRIDGES

The famous U.K. department store consistently offers customers a rich array of new experiences. In 2014, it announced record operating profits of £150 million, up 12.3% on the previous year.

THE MUSEUM OF EVERYTHING

In 2011, art project The Museum of Everything launched an exhibition in the store. Over 400 drawings, paintings, and sculptures by self-taught artists with disabilities were displayed. Inside, a Films of Everything display showed the artists at work in their studios.

EDIBLE CRAZY GOLF COURSE

May 2012 saw culinary architects Bompas and Parr install a pop-up nine-hole edible crazy golf course on the roof of the store. The course featured giant cakes, representing famous London landmarks, including Tower Bridge and Nelson's Column.

WORLD'S FIRST DEPARTMENT STORE CINEMA

Also in 2014 the store partnered with the Everyman Cinema to launch a new movie theater on the ground floor of its Oxford Street flagship. The first 12 films to be screened were chosen by influential fashion designers including Marc Jacobs and Paul Smith.

FESTIVAL OF IMAGINATION

In 2014, the store hosted a six-week Festival of Imagination. Alongside displays of innovative and prototype products, artists, writers, and innovators were invited to speak in the in-store Imaginarium, created by designer Rem Koolhaas.

CONNECTION AND COMMUNITY

As we've seen above, businesses that have shifted their thinking toward "creating with" rather than "selling to" have thrived. Underlying that is a key truth about people: alongside the drive toward *self*-actualization is a desire to feel part of something bigger than themselves.

SOCIAL VALUE

Warren Buffett noted, "price is what you pay, value is what you get." Nowhere is the new mind-set around *social* value more honed than in the Collaborative Economy. Here, new collaborative models enable customers to deal directly with other people, while the brand—nay, the *platform*—acts as facilitator rather than traditional provider. For "users" (the people formerly known as customers) these models offer a more meaningful consumerism, one that allows them to be active participants rather than mere passive consumers.

Once people experience this sense of connection, it quickly starts to feel normal, if not expected. Cue the exponential growth of the best Collaborative Economy platforms. It took Airbnb (the poster child of the movement) three years—from launch in 2008 to 2011—to see 5 million nights booked via its platform. The next 5 million nights were booked in less than a year.

RISING TRUST

Of course, participation in the Collaborative Economy requires trust in strangers. But trust in peer-to-peer models will only increase as the volume of participants increases, causing reputation ratings and other indicators of trustworthiness to become more reliable.

What's more, the combination of two-way rating and genuine connection means the peer-to-peer experience is often valuable in new ways for those supplying, too. Witness the many Airbnb hosts who share tips about their favorite local experiences with guests.

A POSITIVE CONSUMERISM

So where is all this leading?

Will all peer-to-peer services succeed (or even survive)? No. The winner-take-all network effects of platform business models means many will fail. But those that win will win big, and in the process change the way participants think about consumerism, value, and even themselves.

That's the revolutionary power that the Collaborative Economy can wield, by reducing the profit motive to just one driver of value among many—connection, experience, and more. This is extremely challenging to conventional businesses, which struggle to entertain, let alone compete on, measures of non-financial value.

Ultimately, and as with GUILT-FREE CONSUMPTION, the Collaborative Economy is liberating customers to feel good about their consumption. When "consuming" means participating in networks that are both personally and socially valuable, then far from holding back, customers feel free—if not duty bound—to dive in and embrace that more meaningful and positive consumerism!

BLABLACAR

So-called because of the "chattiness" factor* of its users, BlaBlaCar is a textbook example of the multiple new drivers, motivations, and expectations at play in the Collaborative Economy.

BlaBlaCar is a French ride-sharing platform that allows users to "sell" (at cost) the empty seats in their car on long-distance journeys. The service raised $100 million in July 2014, and by 2015 its members were sharing over 2 million rides per month in 18 countries. It perfectly illustrates two key features of the Collaborative Economy:

First, trust is the essential ingredient. Online communities have revolutionized the level of trust people can place in strangers. In 2012, BlaBlaCar polled its users and found that members with completed profiles were more trusted than neighbors, second only to friends and family.

Second, people have diverse motives for participating. Users reported their reasons for using BlaBlaCar as: saving money (cited by 85 percent of users), but also friendliness (52 percent), the environment (40 percent), sharing (35 percent), and more.

The convergence of these two forces is creating a "customer" experience with new participant expectations—of *more for less*.

As well as disclosing whether they smoke or will carry pets, both drivers and passengers rate how talkative they are—or are comfortable being!

> **Where there is trust, there can be collaboration. There can be value. This is not an incremental change to society . . . it's a disruptive change. Nothing will ever be the same. The building block of society, interpersonal trust, has been transformed from a scarce into an abundant resource. Our potential to collaborate and create value is also transformed.**

Frédéric Mazzella, CEO, BlaBlaCar

THE EXPECTATION CYCLE

Now that all three strands of the Expectation Economy have been laid out, we can step back and view it in its entirety.

The consumer arena we've outlined might seem an intimidating place for innovators. But for customers, the Expectation Economy is about increasing excitement, opportunity, diversity, and value.

Expectations of rising quality, positive impact, and personal expression mean that people are justifiably enthusiastic participants in an ever-accelerating cycle of expectation, consumption, meaningful impact, and yet more consumption.

In summary:

[a] Customers can now be confident that they can get the highest quality available in every purchase and experience.

[b] This is set against an expectation that quality is rising and that the new will be even better.

[c] Seeking out the best of the new, customers gravitate toward CLEAN SLATE BRANDS. That often means consumption of more sustainable, ethical, community-focused, and healthy products and services from

newer brands with contemporary values baked in to their operations.

[d] This results in greater self-actualization, as customers find themselves more closely aligned with their deeply held values: namely, not being responsible for negatively impacting themselves, other people, or the planet.

[e] This pushes customers back to the beginning of the cycle, in the expectation that yet more consumption of that which is newer—and "better"—will mean even more positive impact.

Of course, this is a stylized model of a perfect Expectation Economy at work. We're not saying that all real-world consumption is this simple. The real-life picture is made more complex by all kinds of other motives, contingencies, and realities, both on the customer and business side.

But the trend is undeniable: this fundamental cycle is present in—and underpins—an increasing amount of customer behavior today. And, as we'll explore in the next section, using trends will enable you to understand the secret forces behind many of the contemporary consumer arena's most exciting businesses and enable you to anticipate—and contribute to—the next phase in this cycle of rising quality, positive impact, and personal expression.

> NEXT

Having read this chapter, you now:

[1] Know that the Expectation Economy means ever-
     higher customer expectation, applied ruthlessly to
     every purchasing decision;

[2] Understand the three fundamental strands of
     accelerating expectation: rising quality, positive
     impact, and personal expression; and

[3] Understand how those three strands work in concert
     to create the Expectation Cycle.

....

Next, let's take a look at the fundamentals of consumer
trends and start to see how harnessing these trends can
provide the answers you need to meet the challenges
posed in this chapter. Onward!

....

SCAN

THE OVERWHELM IS THE OPPORTUNITY.

So relentless hyper-competition and accelerating consumer expectations have you constantly playing catch-up.

Consumer trends take the overwhelming nature of these forces and turn them to your advantage. Understanding and tracking trends gives you a handle on the information onslaught and a framework through which to understand rapid change.

Let's start by unpacking what trends are and how to spot, track, and process them in a meaningful way.

[SCAN]

TRENDS 101

Where to start with
consumer trends.

The moment you say "trends" you step into a minefield of potential confusion. Are you talking about aging populations, the rise of China, or the next breakout digital device? Or are you about to forecast next season's hottest color?

Somewhat unsurprisingly, consumer trends are about consumers: how they behave, what they want, and how they view the world around them.

More importantly for business professionals, trends *unlock opportunities*. Understanding change—in people's behaviors, attitudes, and expectations—better places you to deliver what they want, not only now but in the future, too.

So, let's get going and look at the fundamental elements of trends.

TRENDS DEFINED

What we mean when
we talk about trends.

A CONSUMER TREND IS
A NEW MANIFESTATION
AMONG PEOPLE—IN
BEHAVIOR, ATTITUDE,
OR EXPECTATION—
OF A FUNDAMENTAL
HUMAN NEED, WANT,
OR DESIRE.

A new behavior. A new attitude or opinion. A new expectation. Any of these can form the basis of a consumer trend.

Underneath our definition lies a model that juxtaposes multiple dimensions of external change against human nature, which, at its most fundamental, doesn't change.

But it's not enough to simply understand a trend. You want to know where and how trends will emerge and crucially, which opportunities they will present to you.

THE SECRET TO SPOTTING
TRENDS AND BEING READY
TO ACT ON THE OPPORTUNITIES
THEY PRESENT YOU LIES
IN IDENTIFYING POINTS OF
TENSION BETWEEN WHAT
PEOPLE WANT AND WHAT IS
CURRENTLY AVAILABLE.

THE FUNDAMENTAL TREND ELEMENTS

Three core components. One point of tension to identify and resolve.

There are three fundamental elements that drive all trends:

[1]   Basic needs

[2]   Drivers of change

[3]   Innovations

The secret ingredient of trends, however, isn't actually any one of these elements. Rather, it's the tension created as the three elements interact with one another.

This tension can best be identified by understanding customer expectations and by looking for gaps between what customers want—both now and in the future—and what they are currently being offered.

We'll go into this idea in more detail in the pages that follow (and indeed, throughout much of the next chapter), but ultimately understanding this enables you to hit the sweet spot of trend-driven innovation when you beat customers' expectations and resolve this tension.

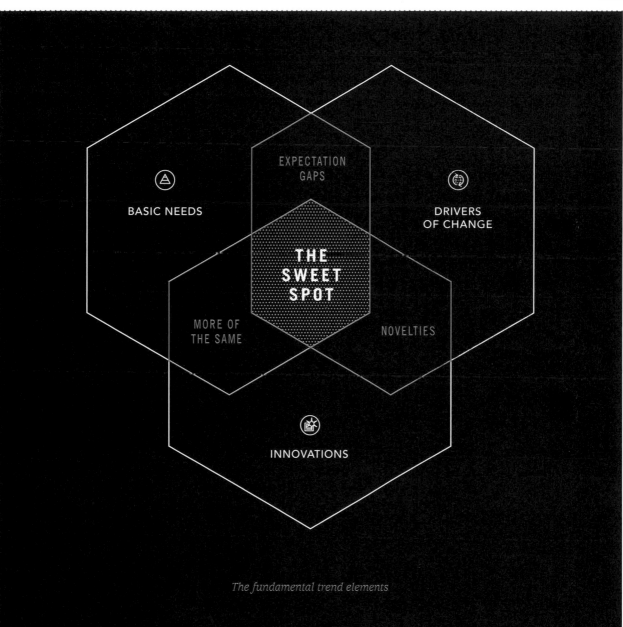

The fundamental trend elements

[1]

BASIC NEEDS
AND WANTS

We're all human. Trends—and behavior more broadly—are ultimately rooted in our basic, fundamental, rarely-if-ever-changing human needs, wants, and desires.

Identifying these basic needs and desires isn't rocket science or even deep social science! They are the forces that have been shaping personal and social relations for centuries, if not millennia. Think about the emotions and passions that drive characters in the great works of literature. Or just listen to popular music, or watch any trashy movie. The same themes crop up again and again, precisely because they are so universally relevant and timeless.

Identifying underlying human needs is central to spotting and/or understanding any consumer trend.

Where to start when looking for these basic human needs, wants, and desires? How about the ones on the opposite page?

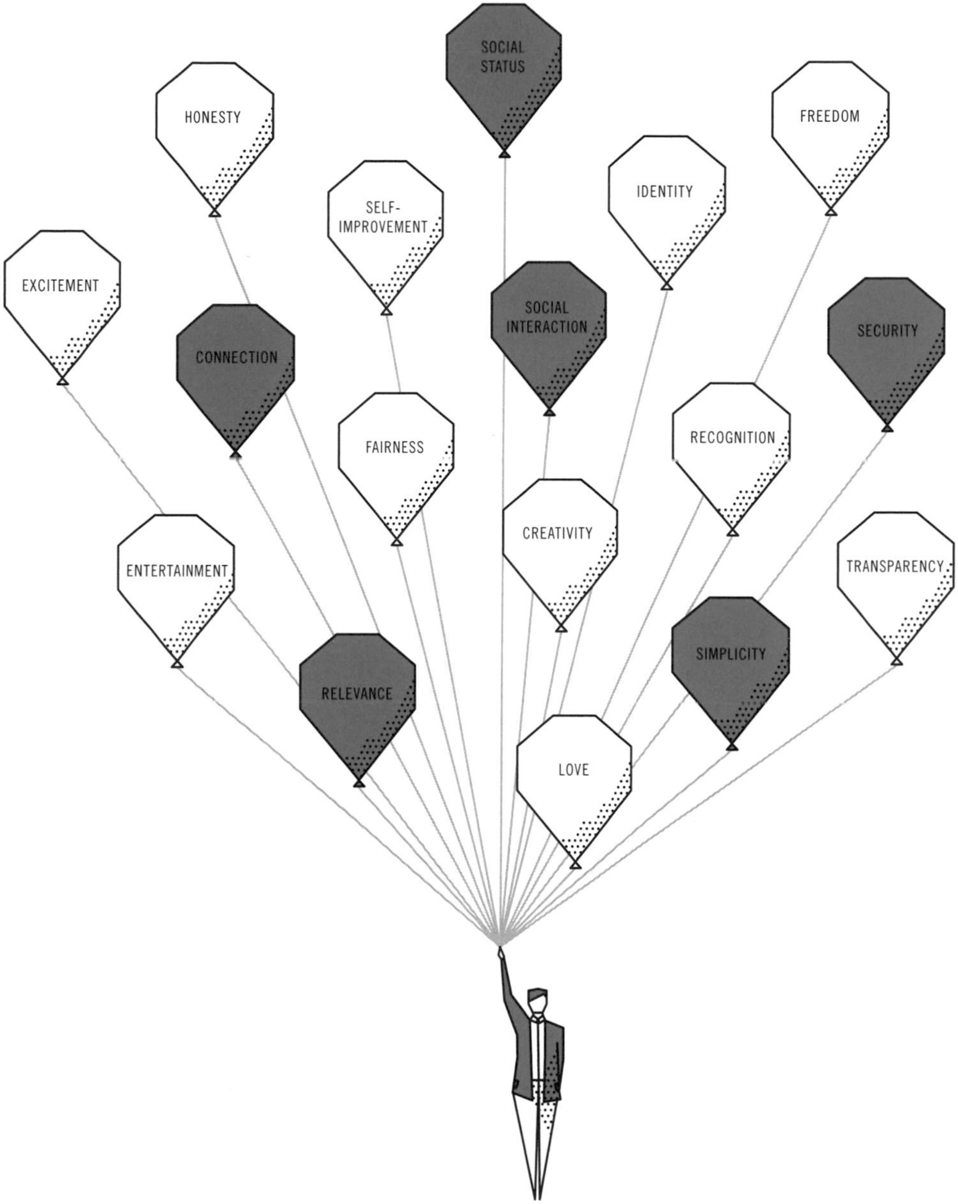
SOCIAL STATUS
HONESTY
FREEDOM
SELF-IMPROVEMENT
IDENTITY
EXCITEMENT
SOCIAL INTERACTION
SECURITY
CONNECTION
FAIRNESS
RECOGNITION
CREATIVITY
ENTERTAINMENT
TRANSPARENCY
SIMPLICITY
RELEVANCE
LOVE

[2]

DRIVERS OF CHANGE: SHIFTS AND TRIGGERS

On the other hand, there are no trends without change. Savvy and switched-on business professionals constantly ask "what's changing?" and look at how it might be possible to service people's basic human needs and wants in novel, exciting, and better ways.

To analyze change, think in terms of Shifts and Triggers.

Shifts are the long-term, macro changes (such as urban transition, aging populations, and climate change) that play out across years or even decades. While not consumer trends themselves, these shifts do and will continue to shape both the nature and direction of consumer trends.

Triggers are more immediate changes that drive the emergence of a trend. These can include specific technologies, political events, economic shocks, environmental incidents, and more. For example, the Snowden/NSA revelations caused many to re-evaluate the trade-offs they were making when sharing their personal data with "free" online services.

Identifying drivers of change:

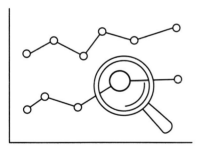

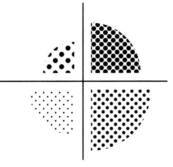

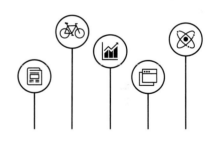

DATA

Rapid growth or sudden shifts are worth attention, no matter how small the absolute numbers. Don't ignore something just because it is 1 percent of the market (or even of your sales or users). If it doubles, then quickly doubles again, ask why.

FRAMEWORKS

Strategic frameworks can be useful tools to analyze external change. Check out the PESTLE model (Political, Economic, Social, Technological, Legal, and Environmental) and its various adaptations.

NONCONSUMER TRENDS

Other types of trends, from what's popular on social networks to hot new product categories, can also shine a light on social change and inform your thinking about consumer trends (see Section 2.2 for more on nonconsumer trends).

[3]

INNOVATIONS

Innovations aren't trends. But without examples of customer-facing innovations tapping into it, a trend can't be said to exist fully (it's either a futurist's flight of fancy or an as yet unvalidated opportunity).

You can't identify a trend for more irreverent, "human" brands without businesses like Ben & Jerry's or Old Spice delighting customers. You can't describe the rise of the "on-demand economy" without the existence and rapid growth of services like Uber or Instacart. You can't have a zoo without animals!

So, the third element of every trend is innovations: the startups, new products, services, experiences, and campaigns that are resolving points of customer tension and creating new levels of customer expectation.

Of course, when it comes to trends, there are "good" and "bad" innovations. On-trend innovations (shown previously) will be those that hit the sweet spot and cater to people's basic needs while anticipating or responding to external change.

[FEATURE]

TRENDS VS. FADS

We're always asked what the difference is. In short: what we do is a trend; how we do it can be a fad. Trends arise when external change unlocks new ways to serve fundamental human needs. The specific products and services that people use may indeed be mere fads, even those that sit firmly in the on-trend sweet spot.

Take a service like Tinder. The Facebook-powered mobile dating app, where users can only message each other if they both "swipe right" to signal mutual interest, exploded in popularity during 2013 and 2014, announcing in October 2014 that it was seeing over 1 billion swipes and 12 million matches a *day*.

Zoom out a little: the web unlocked new ways to serve the age-old desire for human connection; next, the convergence of social networks and smartphones helped shift expectations around instant connection and social gratification from the online world into people's real offline social lives, too. *Those are trends*, with Tinder as a hugely successful and novel example.

Is the service a fad, or will single young urbanites still be swiping furiously in 2025? Who knows? We don't have a crystal ball. It's not important anyway: trends *aren't* about the success or failure of individual innovations later in this chapter.

However, will the desire for instant connection and social gratification continue? Yes.

Will there continue to be exciting new opportunities for those who cater to that desire? Absolutely!

EMERGING EXPECTATIONS

The target of every
on-trend innovation.

The three fundamental elements—basic needs, external change, and innovations—will help you *understand* trends. But sensing where and how these come together to form new levels of customer expectation will help you *act* on trends. That's because identifying what the people embracing the brands, products, and services that embody the trend now want and even expect is the best way to spot the potential opportunities within a trend.

We've already seen how customers have increasingly high expectations of rising quality, positive impact, and personal expression.

Another example of emerging expectations is evident around online piracy of media content. In 1999, Napster took advantage of faster and more widespread Internet access (a prolific driver of change) to set expectations around infinite choice and free access to media. It took until 2008 for Spotify to offer customers a legitimate outlet for that expectation, finally supported by a music industry

WHAT DO THE PEOPLE EMBRACING THE BRANDS, PRODUCTS, AND SERVICES THAT EMBODY A TREND NOW WANT AND EVEN EXPECT?

willing to tolerate free streaming. Netflix axed its limit on the volume of content its subscribers could stream the same year. It had taken nearly a decade to resolve the tension and resulting expectations that digital distribution and (illegal) file-sharing had created.

Clearly there are many factors at work (others tried to launch streaming services during that decade). But identifying an unmet customer expectation will make it clear which points of tension you should focus on resolving.

The next chapter looks in detail at how you can draw insights from other organizations' innovation efforts to anticipate what *your* customers will want.

What if you can't see any innovations that are catering to the new customer expectation you've identified? You might just be close to the holy grail of trends: when it is your innovation that *starts* a trend by setting a new level for customer expectations that other innovators have to work to meet!

> NEXT

Having read this chapter, you now:

[1] Understand the three fundamental elements of a trend: basic human needs, change (both longer-term shifts and short-term triggers), and innovations;

[2] Can identify points of tension and emerging customer expectations, which are where the key opportunities lie when it comes to trends; and

[3] Know how to start a trend!

....

Next, learn how to apply this model to spot emerging consumer trends via an analysis of new business innovation.

....

WATCH BUSINESSES FIRST, CUSTOMERS SECOND

The counterintuitive secret to customer-centricity.

As everyone from Henry Ford to Steve Jobs knew, turning to customers for insights about their future desires is limiting at best, and can be downright misleading.

If there's one secret to trend watching, however, it is that you *can* know what customers will start to want. Not by asking them, but by looking at the businesses and products that people are lavishing love and attention on now.

These are the businesses—from well-known leaders such as Apple and Whole Foods, to niche brands such as Zady, a "lifestyle destination for conscious consumers," to new products such as the Pebble smartwatch, which, as we saw previously, raised $10.2 million in 30 days on Kickstarter—that drive the Expectation Economy by triggering points of tension and creating new expectations among consumers.

Indeed, it's because of the Expectation Economy that you should aim to build a culture of customer-*centered* innovation, not customer-*led* innovation.

Customer-led cultures are reactive and too self-consciously explicit about putting the customer first. Customer-centered cultures, on the other hand, are grounded in a deeply empathetic understanding of customer needs and wants, but also grant an organization the freedom to make the unexpected and often unasked-for leaps forward that will lead to long-term success.

Let's find out how. . . .

FUTURE VISION

Business innovation
as a source of future-
focused insight.

Businesses typically rely on two main sources of customer insight. There's data science, where the bigger the data collection and analysis the better. Then there are the social sciences, where deeper and richer is better.

Both are valid. Both focus on customers. However, subscribe to the model of trends being driven by three fundamental components—basic human needs and wants, external change, and innovations—and you'll find four clear reasons why it's smarter to look to businesses first, customers second when it comes to generating future-focused insights:

- **Expectation Transfer** and the porous nature of customer experience.
- **Bets on the Future** and tapping the wisdom of the business crowd for customer insight.
- **Spotting vs. Creating** and why, when it comes to trends, spotting *is* creating.
- **Revolution from Evolution** and how innovation-led insights can inspire radical progress.

62

[1/4]

EXPECTATION TRANSFER

When it comes to customer needs, wants, and expectations, tension is created through experience.

Consumers use Apple devices and enjoy the quality finish and the seamlessness of them "just working." They walk into an H&M store to find racks of "good enough" quality clothing at rock bottom prices. They travel economy on Singapore Airlines and experience first-class service.

The challenge facing businesses is that these experiences don't simply sit neatly within customers' mobile/ fashion/retail/travel mental silos (as they do in the minds of many business professionals).

Instead, someone riding in a car will wish the in-car entertainment system was as intuitive to use as their iPhone. Someone browsing beauty products will expect to find that sweet spot of price and quality. Someone stopping for a coffee will bristle at anything less than first-class customer service.

Indeed, once people have experienced Apple's design, H&M's affordability, or Singapore Airlines' level of service, it's hard to tolerate "normal" (i.e., lower) standards.

The scariest part of this whole scenario for businesses is that with information traveling more freely than ever, it creates an almost universal familiarity with the standards set by the best-in-class. This means customers' expectations are frequently raised without them having even personally experienced "the best," but merely through *knowing* what standard the "best" represents.

[2/4]

BETS ON THE FUTURE

Every new business venture is a bet on the future that has been put out into the market in order to cater to both current and anticipated customer needs and wants. Using innovations to spot trends therefore allows you to tap the collective intelligence of the business crowd for your future-focused customer insight. Look for multiple actors (preferably in a variety of sectors and/or markets) that are placing similar bets. Analyze these bets through the lens of the fundamental needs and wants that underpin them, and you can draw powerful insights on where customers are headed.

For example during 2014: Intel committed to remove "conflict minerals" from the production of its processors; electric car pioneer Tesla stated that it would not initiate patent lawsuits against anyone using their technology in good faith; drugstore chain CVS removed cigarettes from its stores, despite their sales generating over $2 billion in annual revenue.

These moves appear unconnected at first. But for trend watchers, to witness businesses voluntarily and pre-emptively making certain sacrifices is an interesting signal. These businesses were placing bets that "doing the right thing" (environmentally, socially, or for people's health) would be the right economic decision too.

And while the results of these specific bets remain to be seen, the repeated nature of them should at the very least encourage you to question if you should be placing a similar bet, too.

USING INNOVATIONS TO
SPOT TRENDS ALLOWS
YOU TO TAP INTO THE
COLLECTIVE INTELLIGENCE
OF THE BUSINESS CROWD.

[3/4]

SPOTTING VS. CREATING

Of course, you might ask, "Is looking at business innovation to assess where customers are headed forward-thinking enough?" In other words, do businesses *respond* to customer needs and wants, or *create* them?

It's a valid question and the truth is: businesses do both.

Even innovations from the earliest pioneers will only succeed if they address certain unmet needs or cater to new behaviors. As such, these innovations are *responding* to consumer behavior, at least initially.

However, once certain customers' needs and wants are satisfied in a novel way and the innovation becomes more widely experienced or known, then the initially pioneering brands and innovations quickly *create* new customer expectations (both in other people and, more importantly, in other industries and markets, via the expectation transfer process described above).

Take for example the pioneering U.S.-based eco-friendly cleaning product and personal care brand Seventh Generation. Driven by a belief that a more sustainable approach to business was essential, in the early 1990s it placed what turned out to be a winning bet on the future. As founder Jeffrey Hollender says, he was "solving a problem that people didn't know existed."

As more and more people became aware of the underlying problem, the expectation—demand, even— for sustainable solutions increased. This then fueled a virtuous cycle in which the scale of the winning nature of Seventh Generation's bet also then increased, too.

Since then, a combination of ever-greater awareness and the continued success of more environmentally responsible brands has driven an even greater expectation of—and even higher demand for—eco-friendly alternatives in almost every product category. And this demand is being serviced by a host of brands, from Chipotle (with its fast-but-responsible-food) to Tesla (with its all-electric sports cars) to Zady (with its locally produced "slow fashion" output). Indeed, there continue to be endless opportunities to create new environmentally and socially responsible businesses. Jeffrey Hollender's latest venture is Sustain, a condom brand that takes a full-spectrum approach to ethical and ecological standards, from using certified fair trade and pesticide-free latex to donating 10 percent of its pretax profits to female-focused health and family planning services.

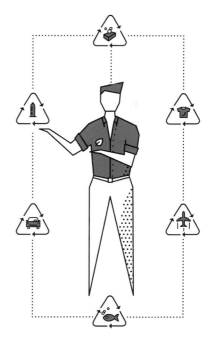

[4/4]

REVOLUTION FROM EVOLUTION

If, however, it's the businesses that respond most rapidly to emerging customer expectations that end up creating trends, then surely the answer to getting ahead is to get ever closer to customers, either via data or social science? Not so fast:

On the quantitative side, while more/better/faster data can lead to valuable insights, data-driven innovation is often incremental in nature. Data is fantastic at validation and optimization, but bad at generating the radical and unconventional connections that underpin many successful innovations.

On the qualitative side, in reality it's not as simple as a pioneering innovator responding to customers' neatly expressed needs and wants. After all, it's impossible to go back and find "pure" customer needs and wants that haven't been shaped through experience and awareness of existing products.

Spotting the innovations that are exciting customers and analyzing them using the fundamental elements of trends is also disruptively faster and cheaper than deep ethnographic fieldwork. Plus, insights drawn from a diverse range of innovations in a variety of markets and sectors will be both novel *and* robust.

That's not to say that data-driven innovation and ethnographic research aren't valuable. Far from it. The insights they generate can be the difference between success or failure. But you shouldn't rely exclusively on these two approaches. Instead, look to complement them with customer

> **Our job is to figure out what they're going to want before they do. . . . People don't know what they want until you show it to them. That's why I never rely on market research. Our task is to read things that are not yet on the page.**
>
> – Steve Jobs

insights generated from watching trends and innovations.

Finally, remember that even the most visionary innovators don't conjure something up from nothing. All innovators build on, adapt, extend, combine, remix, and redeploy things that already exist. Seventh Generation wasn't the first eco-friendly cleaning and personal care brand. Walmart wasn't the first supermarket chain. Kickstarter wasn't the first crowdfunding platform. The iPhone certainly wasn't the first web-enabled cell phone. But all resolved meaningful tensions and set new customer expectations (which then created new points of tension for their competitors' customers).

Indeed, understand why game-changing business innovations are exciting customers—and extend that to identifying broader trends—and you'll be able to consistently identify the next wave of (as-yet-unmet) customer needs and the promising new business opportunities that they present.

INNOVATION CLUSTERS AND TRENDS

Let's now run through *exactly* how to identify consumer trends:

[1] Look for "clusters" of multiple innovations that indicate a number of actors putting similar bets on the future *and* that are creating new levels of customer expectation.

[2] Don't limit your search to product innovation. We look for four types (see opposite). These are, of course, neater in theory than in practice! For example, in early 2015 Marriott Hotels launched an initiative offering guests at selected hotels and resorts free use of GoPro cameras to capture their holiday memories. Guests were encouraged to share their content across social media using the hashtags #travelbrilliantly and #viajegenial in order to be featured on the brand's dedicated site and win prizes. This innovation spans all the four types: supporting the *vision* of travel as being about memorable experiences, tapping into a free, crowdsourced *model* that is powered by a complementary rental *service*, in order to generate authentic *marketing* messages.

[3] The more diverse the range of innovations you spot, the more reliable your insights about future customer needs and wants. Look for innovations that show how the trend is playing out in different contexts. How are startups catering to the trend? How does that differ from big multinationals?

We'll explore this in more detail in the next chapter by showing how seemingly disparate innovations in different industries and markets can be used to identify emerging consumer trends.

Four types of innovation:

VISION
How are the shifts driving the trend manifested in the long-term visions of companies at the forefront of the trend?

BUSINESS MODEL
Is the trend unlocking whole new business models?

PRODUCT/SERVICE/ EXPERIENCE
What new products and services are emerging as a result of the trend?

MARKETING
How are brands reflecting the trend in their marketing and campaigns? How are consumers responding?

THE BUTTERFLY EFFECT

Don't dismiss small, niche, or seemingly "ridiculous" innovations.

You can witness powerful early signals about where customer expectations are headed by looking at extreme cases. Consider the following examples:

Miya's Sushi, a restaurant in New Haven, Connecticut, offers a sushi menu featuring only items made from nonnative, invasive species that are threatening the shellfish that the local fishing economy relies on. Thus eating (and enjoying) these dishes offers customers a sense of positive impact and totally reverses the quandary many people find themselves in when it comes to eating sustainably sourced seafood.

Belgian fashion brand Honest By was launched by Bruno Pieters, an ex-Hugo Boss art director, in 2012. The label takes an extreme approach to transparency, publishing full information about material and supplier sourcing, shows exactly where and how the items are produced, and even gives an itemized breakdown of the material, labor, and distribution costs (and therefore full details of the wholesale and retail markups).

Google announced that Project Ara (its modular cell phone development initiative) would pilot in Puerto Rico in 2015. Customers can purchase a central base unit and can then add, replace, and upgrade specific modular components (such as a new camera unit) individually rather than needing to purchase an entirely new device.

Will these concepts become standard business practice? Unlikely, at least in the short term. But they *do* give valuable information about certain customers' needs and wants. And, as we've shown, even customers who don't demand such extreme levels of sustainability, transparency, or flexibility will start to have their expectations raised by the mere knowledge that there *are* businesses that are offering such benefits. In the same way that famously the flutter of a butterfly's wings can contribute to a hurricane on the other side of the world, so too can a small, local sushi restaurant contribute to the shifting expectations of your customers.

Indeed, whether you like or are excited by an innovation—or even think it makes sense—is irrelevant.

Too often senior (in both senses of the word!) professionals dismiss things that appear too niche or frivolous. From Twitter to Snapchat, Netflix to Airbnb, the online world shows that concepts that can seem half-baked, if not downright bizarre at first, can quickly spread beyond their initial audiences and reach millions.

Don't dismiss novel concepts that are exciting people, even if they

might seem strange or irrelevant to you. Try and understand *why* other people are embracing a new concept. Then think how you could take the underlying insight and run with it.

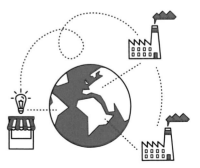

FAILURE

And why it's irrelevant.

Looking at clusters of innovations can provide powerful signals into future customer needs, wants, and expectations. But don't let skeptics question the insights you draw should an example fail. Just as an isolated innovation isn't itself a trend, trying to draw broad conclusions based on the success or failure of individual innovations (or even whole businesses) won't work either.

A single example is simply one data point, a manifestation of the underlying trend within a specific context, for specific customers, in a specific market and sector.

There are simply too many variables (execution, culture, logistics, financing, and more) at work to draw conclusions about entire trends from one or even a handful of examples.

Plenty of peer-to-peer startups failed in recent years. But try telling the founders—and users—of Airbnb that this invalidates the ongoing trend toward peer-to-peer consumerism, when on New Year's Eve 2014 the service saw 550,000 guests stay in properties booked via the site, up from 2,000 just five years previously.

Indeed, there are endless examples of business innovations that failed, despite being favorably aligned with underlying trends. The lesson from all this? Find clusters of multiple and diverse innovations, extract the underlying customer-centered insight, and look beyond the success or failure of a single innovation.

[FEATURE]
FAILURE GALLERY

While these initiatives stalled, the trends (and opportunities) behind them live on.

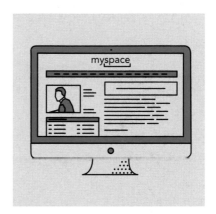

WEBVAN

The online world has its fair share of spectacular flameouts that for multiple reasons failed to resonate or stick with consumers. One of the most notable was online grocer Webvan, which went from a $375 million IPO in 1999 to bankruptcy in 2001. Meanwhile, over in the U.K., Ocado followed a similar (if less ambitious) business model, went public in 2010 after eight years of operations, and had a market capitalization of approximately $4 billion at the end of 2014.

MYSPACE

The social media behemoth of its time (it was the most popular website in the U.S. in July 2006) went from being bought by News Corp. in 2005 for $580 million to being sold to a consortium including Justin Timberlake for just $35 million a mere six years later. Of course, during that time, social networks exploded to new levels of popularity, as shown by the mere 1.4 *billion* people that log onto Facebook every month.

WATCH BUSINESSES FIRST, CUSTOMERS SECOND:
FAILURE GALLERY

BURGER KING

In the fall of 2013, Burger King looked to tap into the trend for healthy eating by launching Satisfries, french fries with 30 percent fewer calories and 40 percent less fat. However, by mid-2014, executives were admitting that the option would be removed from two-thirds of the chain's U.S. outlets after failing to find favor with customers. Does this mean customers aren't embracing healthy fast food? The success of chains such as Lyfe, where all menu items are under 600 calories, suggests otherwise. Founded by an ex-McDonald's executive, the restaurant chain expanded from a single Palo Alto outlet in 2011 to 14 outlets by the end of 2014.

MATTEL

Mattel opened a six-story flagship store in Shanghai in March 2009, also creating Ling, a localized version of its eponymous doll. However, slow sales resulted in the store closing within two years. Does that mean that all flagship stores and localized retail strategies won't win over Chinese customers? Of course not! Indeed, Mattel has since relaunched in China with a lower-priced violin soloist doll, better tailored to the aspirations of Chinese girls (and their parents).

CAR2GO

Carsharing service car2go
(a subsidiary of automotive giant
Daimler AG) enables customers to
rent vehicles by the minute, without
having to return them to the original
pickup location. The service closed
in London within 18 months of
launch, despite signing up over
1 million customers in the 29 other
cities it operated in as of February
2015. However, despite this failure,
rival manufacturer BMW launched
its similar DriveNow service in
London in December 2014,
observing that the British capital
was the largest European market for
Zipcar, the longer-term carsharing
service.

GOOGLE

Google Wallet launched in 2011
promising to move U.S. customers
away from plastic and toward a
world where they could pay by
swiping their NFC-enabled phones
at the checkout. While not an
outright failure, by late 2014, the
service hadn't entered mainstream
customer consciousness.
Meanwhile, Starbucks reported that
their customers had made 7 million
mobile payments per week in the
final quarter of 2014.

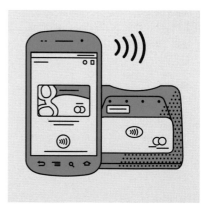

WHERE TO SPOT TRENDS

A modern "bibliography."

There's never been a more exciting time for eager, trend-driven innovators to be in business.

In a world where an almost infinite number of smart professionals and amateurs are not only spotting, observing, thinking, and innovating, but also putting their findings and insights online for all to see, deliciously valuable resources have never been more accessible, and many of them are free or dirt cheap. So, stop complaining about information overload and instead celebrate the incredible wealth of resources at your fingertips!

On the coming pages you'll find our go-to list of sources that we use to spot the new products, services, and businesses that are redefining consumer expectations and to uncover supersmart thinking on where customers, societies, and businesses are headed next.

 Head online for a full list of the sources that we're currently reading.

Traditional media
For all their struggles, daily newspapers and monthly magazines do still contain an astonishing number of relevant, well-researched, and well-written pieces on the latest local, regional, and global social, cultural, and business happenings.

Niche/specialist media
Then there is the vast universe of publications, newsletters, and blogs, providing a never-ending stream of information about every conceivable interest and subculture. Another tip: airline magazines always offer great snapshots of novel global happenings.

Business publications
Industries and sectors of particular note include technology and innovation, small business, marketing and advertising, retail, consultancies, designers, and architects.

Company newsfeeds
These are ideal for press releases about new offerings and initiatives. Agency blogs often contain case studies and reflections on client projects. Startup accelerators can also be a great source to discover new and disruptive concepts.

Social media
Harvest influencers' newsfeeds for valuable insights. The public and directly accessible network of people available via Facebook, Twitter, LinkedIn, Instagram, and more is hard to beat, if well curated.

WATCH BUSINESSES FIRST, CUSTOMERS SECOND:
WHERE TO SPOT TRENDS

 Alerts
Set up a Google alert for "[your country's/ industry's] first," "plans to launch," or other forward-looking phrases and watch the results roll in.

 Spotter network
We source a large portion of our content through our dedicated global network of trend spotters. While obviously it's our business to do so, anyone can create, gather, inspire, and lead a group of like-minded individuals nowadays. If you're within a big global company, why not start internally? Alternatively, reach out to people you know and set up a group in an existing social network.

 Crowdfunding sites
These offer an incredible window into a live, real-world innovation lab, where customer reaction to products can be validated before they have even been fully realized. Start by checking out Kickstarter and Indiegogo, the two largest sites.

 Conferences and events
Physically attending will help you get hands-on with new technologies. But even when that's not possible, the abundant stream of readily available conference keynotes can let you hear from experts and practitioners for free.

 Thought leaders
Insights from CEOs of game-changing companies are always worth reading, given that they think deeply about the future of the

trends they are tapping into. Also look to venture capitalists and investors, whose very existence depends on their ability to make correct bets on the future.

 Academia
Dive into formal academic research as well as student projects, showcases, and competitions to find new ideas. Many student projects will be very raw, but watch out for those that are commercialized and developed.

 Daily life
Listen and observe what people are raving about. Take an interest in the world around you. Browse shops and wander through malls. Travel as much as possible. Watch popular media.

Comedy and satire
One final, often-overlooked gold mine: comedy and satire frequently produce perhaps the sharpest insights of all by shining a light on cultural shifts and behaviors in ways that few other sources can match.

THE VARIOUS TYPES OF TRENDS

Macro trends, political and economic trends, technology trends. Fashion and social trends. Then there is what's popular and "trending." So many trends, so little time. . . .

However, these aren't *consumer* trends, in the sense that in themselves they are not new behaviors, attitudes, or expectations. Instead, "trends" such as these and those on the opposite page are often better analyzed via the Shifts and Triggers framework introduced previously.

For example, drones are not a consumer trend. However, the use of drones by businesses and consumers themselves is likely to heighten expectations of ultra-convenience, instant gratification, and being in control, as well as trigger new consumer behavior (like posing for a "dronie").

Low-cost airlines are not a consumer trend. However, the ability to have novel experiences at low cost, the ratcheting up of middle-class lifestyles, and the exposure to global (or at least regional) cultures are increasingly widespread behaviors and set expectations that then underpin many consumer trends.

The aging population is not a consumer trend. But start looking at the products and services a healthier, more active, demanding, design-conscious older generation of customers is embracing, and thinking of the future opportunities that these desires present—and you'll be onto something!

Seven common types of nonconsumer trends:

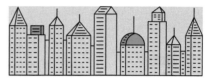

Macro trends
Aging populations / Urbanization

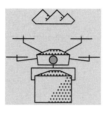

New product categories
Drones / Virtual reality

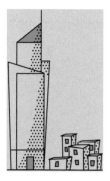

Social, political, and economic trends
Growing economic inequality

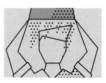

Popular trends
#trending / ALS Ice Bucket Challenge

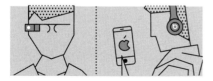

Industry trends
Android vs Apple / Low-cost airlines

Fashion trends
Normcore / Beards

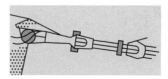

Futurism
Self-driving cars / Intelligent robots

> NEXT

Having read this chapter, you now:

[1] Understand why analyzing business innovations is key to anticipating what customers will want next;

[2] Know the four types of innovations to look out for: vision, business model, product/service, and marketing; and

[3] Have a bank of resources that you can scour for the next wave of expectation-setting innovations.

....

In the following chapters, we'll show how to use this methodology to identify real-world consumer trends, and then how to bring these together into a comprehensive and practical Trend Framework.

....

TRENDS IN THE WILD

Four trends and how we
identified them.

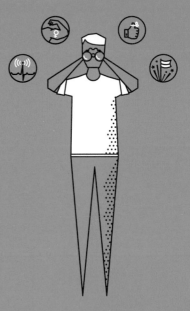

Enough theory, let's see these ideas in action!

The trends featured in the following pages show how we connected the dots between innovations of diverse types—from startups to multinationals, from disruptive new business models to novel products, services, and campaigns—and uncovered a host of promising new consumer trends in the process.

Want more? Find our latest trends at trendwatching.com/trends

INTERNET OF CARING THINGS

Smart objects
designed to protect
and care for people.

Released in October 2013, the Nest Protect is a two-in-one smoke alarm and carbon monoxide detector designed to be more intelligent than traditional devices. A spoken warning (rather than a noisy alarm) allows users to check whether the cause of smoke is serious. If it isn't, they can simply wave at the device to ensure the alarm doesn't activate, while the device also sends warnings about potential hazards or low battery power to an accompanying app.

Also in 2013, football helmet manufacturer Riddell launched its InSite Impact Response System. The smart helmets contain sensors that send an alert to coaches when they detect a significant impact, and medical professionals can then assess the player for signs of concussion.

Automaker Ford released a concept smart car seat in late 2013, too. ECG heart rate sensors can detect mid-journey heart attacks and engage assistance systems, while diabetic drivers can connect to an onboard glucose level monitoring system that alerts them to critical blood sugar level changes.

Then in 2014, Chinese technology giant Baidu released a set of prototype smart chopsticks, containing sensors able to measure the freshness of cooking oil, a common concern for Chinese consumers. The concept was originally created as an April Fool's spoof, but generated such interest that the company's engineers pursued it (read more about this innovative route to market in Chapter 6.

New technologies frequently arouse plenty of excitement. But they can also be powerful triggers for new consumer trends. Take the much-hyped Internet of Things, that is, the phenomenon of connecting objects—rather than just computers and cellphones—to the Internet. Amid all the breathlessness (a smart refrigerator!), we witnessed a subset of devices that had a clear and compelling mission: to actively protect their users' physical and mental well-being.

Here's how we used the fundamental elements to arrive at the INTERNET OF CARING THINGS trend:

- The application of new technologies to age-old and fundamental human needs (in this case, safety).
- Clear drivers of change: from improved efficiency and falling cost of adding wireless connectivity to physical objects to smaller, more personal and precise sensors.
- A compelling case for new expectations. Indeed, after Nest's upgrading of a previous bland and functional device and Riddell's smart football helmet, the question customers will ask when faced with objects *without* a in-built protective function will shortly be "why not?"

The varied nature of the "bets on the future" further supports the trend: the innovations address multiple insecurities (domestic, food contamination, physical injury, reducing motor accidents), the innovations span multiple sectors and markets, and there are multiple indicators of success (Google bought Nest for $3.2 billion, a spoof going viral, the significant and long-term investments made by Ford).

One final insight to take away: as with so many technology-focused trends, the most powerful element in the trend is not the technology itself, but more about how that technology enables innovators to service people's basic needs in new and better ways.

FEMPOWERMENT

The overthrowing of gender stereotypes and promotion of female empowerment.

Facebook COO Sheryl Sandberg launched Lean In, a nonprofit organization to inspire women to achieve their goals in 2014. It partnered with Getty Images to launch an online image library designed to challenge stereotypes of women in stock photo footage. The Lean In Collection features 2,500 images showing women and girls in a positive or powerful light, for example playing soccer and leading business meetings.

Hair care brand Pantene launched a campaign in the Philippines highlighting the different labels given to men and women in the workplace. Where a male executive might be called "persuasive," a female counterpart is called "pushy." A father working late is labeled as "dedicated" while a mother doing the same is branded as "selfish." The campaign attracted so much attention online that the brand turned it into an international media campaign.

July 2014 saw the first graduates from the Lady Mechanic Initiative, a Nigerian NGO sponsored by Coca-Cola that provides women with a three-year training program in automotive engineering and apprenticeships in local car garages.

Launched in late 2014, IAmElemental action figures are designed to reinterpret the traditional action figure while providing positive and empowering role models for young girls. The U.S.-created toys are named for different character attributes, such as Bravery, Energy, and Honesty.

Innovations that reflect changing social norms can be powerful indicators of emerging consumer trends. Clearly women's situations, rights, and opportunities differ enormously around the world. Despite this, we have seen a surge in brands supporting or even initiating challenges to gender stereotypes and female oppression.

Here's how we used the fundamental elements to arrive at the FEMPOWERMENT trend:

- The desire for equality is one of the most basic of human needs.

- Multiple overlapping and converging shifts and triggers, from changing workforce dynamics to modernization and globalization of cultural norms to high-profile positive and negative individual incidents.
- Increasing expectation that business responsibility extends to the full spectrum of social issues.

Note how trends don't respect borders. Deep-rooted human needs are increasingly universal. Meanwhile, the globalization of information means that a campaign can quickly spread globally, as Pantene's did.

Cast a wide net when tracking innovations: important trends will see multiple actors launching new initiatives, from nonprofits to entrepreneurs to the biggest multinationals.

Innovations can be both positive and negative. Challenging the current status quo (as Lean In and Pantene did) can be as clear a signal of a trend as offering a new vision of the future (as Coca-Cola and IAmElemental did).

TRENDS IN THE WILD

FLAWSOME

The awesomeness of
being honest, including
about one's flaws.

We looked earlier at how Domino's tackled the issue of transparency and quality head-on. In a similar fashion, McDonald's Canada released a number of videos on YouTube answering user-submitted questions. In 2012, the chain shared details of how food photographers treated and manipulated products on photo shoots (answering a question about why items bought in-store never looked as juicy and appetizing as those in the photos!). The video received over 10 million views. A follow-up in 2014 gave viewers a tour of a meat processing plant that produces chicken nuggets, in response to a question asking whether Chicken McNuggets contain "pink goop"—a slimy meat product created from industrialized processing.

The Four Seasons luxury hotel chain's website features customer reviews from TripAdvisor and comments from Facebook and Twitter. Comments are placed prominently on hotel pages, and users can click directly through to the external content, often a rarity for luxury brand websites.

Finnish insurance company If has been running its "Kysy Vaikka!" ("Just Ask") initiative since 2012. The company's website features existing customers who've recently made insurance claims. Those featured have agreed to be available from 9 AM to 8 PM via telephone or email to discuss their experience and level of satisfaction. Expectation-raising transparency indeed!

Surprising or counterintuitive initiatives are always interesting to trend watchers. In this case, it was seeing businesses serve up honest and unedited feedback to customers and address controversial issues head-on, steps that have previously often been considered too risky.

Here's how we used the fundamental elements to arrive at the FLAWSOME trend:

- Customers' basic need for honest, reliable information.
- Changes in the perception of business: from disgust at corporate (mis)behavior to the raw immediacy of online culture to the total transparency fostered by the avalanche of readily available reviews and ratings.
- These created an environment in which customers no longer expect businesses to be flawless. In fact, we saw people (whose reactions are now visible on social media) embracing FLAWSOME brands, and perceiving them as still brilliant despite their flaws (or perhaps *because* they acknowledged them in a "human" manner).

When witnessing a counterintuitive move, ask yourself what the organization in question is trying to communicate. And how are customers responding?

Also worth remembering: for every big shift (such as transparency), there will be "smaller" opportunities that innovation-centered trend spotting can identify. We'll explore this idea further and show how to structure a comprehensive Trend Framework in the following chapter.

CELEBRATION NATION

A re-evaluation of local tradition and culture.

Mumbai-based luxury fashion designer Masaba Gupta's House of Masaba has reinvented the traditional Indian sari with quirky, modern motifs and pop art prints that are targeted at young, affluent, urban female customers. Her black-and-white camera print sari has been worn by several Indian Bollywood celebrities.

The Botanique hotel, opened in late 2012 in the city of Campos do Jordão, is one of the most expensive in Brazil, with rates starting at $1,200 a night.

However, Botanique's library is stocked with Brazilian authors, and the food and even the wine list are also all produced locally. This would have been unheard of a few years before, when "local" was seen as downmarket and luxury strongly associated with foreign imports and brands.

Avi Arad, producer of various superhero films including *Fantastic Four*, *Iron Man*, and *Spider-Man*, is making a series of superhero movies about traditional Chinese culture, starting with *Rise of the Terracotta Warriors*. The films are a joint venture with China-based Seven Stars Entertainment.

Turkish soap opera *Muhtesem Yüzyıl (Magnificent Century)* is a historical TV series about the longest reigning sultan of the Ottoman Empire, Suleiman the Magnificent, and his wife Roxelana. The Turkish show is hugely popular with audiences throughout North Africa, the Middle East, and Central and Eastern Europe and has an estimated audience of 200 million viewers.

Connecting tangible business innovations with the larger macro-economic currents is another useful trend-spotting technique. These examples show emerging market audiences recasting symbols of national and cultural heritage and viewing them with pride (where they had previously often been downplayed if not denied as these markets strived to "catch up").

Here's how we used the fundamental elements to arrive at the CELEBRATION NATION trend:

- An appeal to basic needs? Pride and recognition tick those boxes.
- Compelling shifts and triggers: from the macroeconomic shifts described above to the growing affluent, experienced, and increasingly confident younger populations in markets such as China, India, Turkey, and Brazil.

- An emerging tension centered on the disparity between the growing financial power of these "new" economies and the relative lack of modern, exciting home-grown cultural symbols.

Remember to keep your eye on trends once you've initially noticed them. After we had identified the CELEBRATION NATION trend, we then saw a host of innovations that catered to the desire for global audiences to learn about and experience the culture of the new economic superpowers. For example, Budweiser ran a

campaign in 2013 promoting Chinese New Year in New York's Times Square. The campaign was in part aimed at Chinese expatriates and tourists, but also designed to raise awareness of the festival among Americans, too.

The bigger message is that consumer tastes and preferences are shaped by a whole range of factors. Change in one area (economics) will lead to change in other areas (culture). Can you think of other ways consumer behavior will change as a result of the global economic macro-trends that are taking place?

FLAWSOME... FEMPOWERMENT

A quick note on naming trends.

A quick thought on naming trends. We feel it's crucial to describe trends as imaginatively as possible. Sure, we regularly take flak about our names (FLAWSOME? Really?!), but here's why we do it:

Strange names arouse interest, prompt people to sit up and listen, and make them want to know more. A well-chosen name radiates the promise of a story. And if that name is unlike anything else (even if it's a little ridiculous), who can resist the desire to probe a little deeper and not miss out?

Names also create a common language. Teams will rally behind a named concept more easily than behind something generic. And speaking a common language saves team members time—they can refer to a project or trend name and instantly be on the same page.

So just how do we come up with our names? Early on, we were inspired by Faith Popcorn's approach: mix and match two or three words that define the trend, creating a new word that preferably hasn't been used by anyone else (a

quick check on Google will reveal how unique a made-up word is).

So when we saw a number of businesses tackling extreme transparency head-on and being open and honest about their products and services (even if that meant exposing some of their flaws), we bounced some ideas around and came up with flawed + awesome = FLAWSOME.

BUILDING A TREND FRAMEWORK

Why you need one; how to build it; sharing ours.

Now you know exactly how to spot trends by identifying clusters of new business innovations and analyzing them in light of the other two fundamental trend elements—basic human needs and drivers of change—to recognize the customer expectations that are emerging from the interplay between them. This puts you in a great position to anticipate future customer needs, wants, and desires.

However, spotting individual trends is just part of the puzzle. Trends (and the resulting opportunities they unlock) are infinitely more powerful if you have a clear view of how they fit into the bigger picture.

That's where a Trend Framework comes into play. Building a robust and comprehensive framework means you can more effectively and efficiently capture and process the innovations you spot.

Let's examine how to construct one, and show you our Trend Framework as it is currently.

TREND HIERARCHY

From big to small:
Mega-trends. Trends. Innovations.

A good Trend Framework allows you to put almost every innovation you spot into context.

We feed our trend insights into the three main "layers" shown in the pyramid on the opposite page. At the bottom are hundreds of innovations, clusters of which support the middle layer of individual trends. Above this sits the mega-trend* layer.

If our approach to spotting individual trends is bottom up (and driven by clusters of business innovations), then our approach to structuring our Trend Framework is top down (and driven by the big forces shaping the future of the consumer arena at large).

We look at two main forces when assessing our mega-trends:

[1] **Human**. These are the universally relevant human needs and wants that make up the first fundamental element of trend analysis. They include the search for social status, for connection, for self-improvement, for entertainment, for reliable and trusted information, and more.

[2] **Environmental**. The changes in the external environment that are central to the second fundamental element of trend analysis. Examples include increasing transparency, the shifting contours of global economic power, and the blurring of boundaries between producer and consumer thanks to creative technologies and platforms.

Whether internally or externally focused, mega-trends are big, slow-moving currents that remain broadly stable year-on-year, and can be applied across regions, industries, and demographics. People aren't suddenly (if ever) going to stop wanting information or no longer care about the impact of the products they consume.

That's not to say mega-trends don't ever change. In late 2014 we replaced our TRIBES & LIVES mega-trend (which captured trends related to specific customer segments and lifestyles) with the POST-DEMOGRAPHIC mega-trend later in this chapter. This reflected the fact that traditional customer segmentation—via conventional perspectives on gender, income, age, family status, and more—is increasingly inadequate in a world where people are constructing their identities more freely than ever before.

There you have it. Start by identifying clusters of innovations. Analyze these using the fundamental elements to uncover potential new trends. Orient these within a Trend Framework. Too abstract? Let's bring it to life by walking through our Trend Framework as it currently stands.

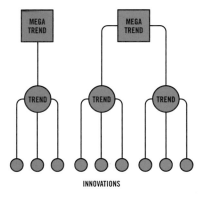

INNOVATIONS

Macro trends, mega-trends, micro trends, mini trends. We admit the world of trend classification is somewhat confused (and confusing!). The truth is, there is no definitive answer, and we're not going to even try to claim one here. In the end it doesn't matter, just as long as you're speaking the same language as other stakeholders.

OUR TREND FRAMEWORK

STATUS SEEKERS

The relentless, ever-present force that underpins almost all consumer behavior.

The desire for recognition and status is a deep and universal human need. People in consumer societies derive much of their social status through the goods, services, and experiences they consume. And with so many choices available in modern economies, consuming becomes as much a statement about who you are, as to what you have.

BETTERMENT

The universal quest for self-improvement.

Show us someone who doesn't aspire to self-improvement. The drive to better oneself can manifest itself in a number of ways, such as the desire for enhanced health, for greater knowledge, and the development of new skills. Businesses, products, and services that satisfy these needs will therefore simply appear "better" than those that don't.

LOCAL LOVE

Why "local" is, and will remain, loved.

Despite globalization, despite online, place still matters. The local world is more tangible, more accessible, more visible, and therefore more "real." Whether driven by a sense of pride, authenticity, convenience, and/or eco-concerns, customers will continue to embrace local products, services, and knowledge.

YOUNIVERSE

Make your consumers the center of their youniverse.

The YOUNIVERSE is each person's consumption realm, where his/her preferences and tastes reign. Cater to an individual's YOUNIVERSE with brilliantly customized products, by enabling and encouraging personal expression, or by offering protection from harm. Whichever route you take, remember: each customer is unique.

OUR TREND FRAMEWORK

EPHEMERAL

Why consumers will embrace the here, the now, and the soon-to-be-gone.

Whether to satisfy their ever-shorter attention spans, their lust for the now, or their craving for real, physical interaction, customers are moving beyond the fixed or static. Instead, they are rushing to collect, record, share, or store as many fleeting moments, experiences, and stories as possible. That's why "time" and its many dimensions should be your next innovation frontier.

Who said business had to be boring?

Surprise. Entertainment. Amusement. People will relish brands that bring some much-needed fun to the business arena. Introducing competitive and participatory games, embracing humor, or celebrating the unexpected will make life—and consumption—less boring and simply more enjoyable.

PLAYSUMERS

JOYNING

The eternal desire for connection, and the many new ways it can be satisfied.

Could there be a more basic need? People are social animals and will forever enjoy coming together, making connections, collaborating, and sharing experiences. The good news? There have never been more opportunities—in both the "real" and virtual worlds—to cater to, benefit from, or facilitate this basic desire.

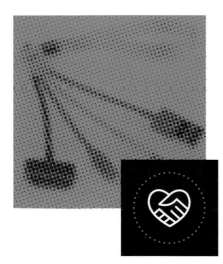

HELPFULL

Be part of the solution, not the problem.

Consumers lead busy, busy lives. Thanks to everything from abundant and limitless choice to the seeming absence of any free time, customers have never felt more overwhelmed. Naturally therefore, innovations, products, and services that make life more convenient, simpler, easier, or seamless will eternally find favor with consumers. Need we waste *your* time by saying more?

OUR TREND FRAMEWORK

BETTER BUSINESS

Why "good" business will be good for business.

Rising numbers of people are aware of the negative impacts that their consumption has on the planet, society, or themselves. Which is why the only truly sustainable, long-term competitive advantage will be solutions that lessen—or eradicate entirely—those negative impacts.

HUMAN BRANDS

Why personality and purpose will mean profit.

Customers are increasingly aware that personality and profit *are* compatible. They will embrace brands with meaning and personality: that are open, honest, generous, have fun, and stand for something—or more importantly, help consumers tell the world what they stand for.

INFOLUST

Why consumers' voracious appetite for (even more) information will only grow.

Forget information overload. People's desire for relevant, useful, timely information is insatiable. It puts them in control. It helps them make the right decisions, or at least makes them feel like they have the power to do so. This is why customers will embrace products, tools, and services that bring them the right information, at the right time, in an understandable, intuitive, and actionable way.

UBITECH

The ever-greater pervasiveness of technology.

Technology will become ever more ubiquitous, universal, and impossible to live without. Why? Quite simply because people will continue to crave (and build their lives around) the unparalleled "superpowers" that technology offers them: perfect and instant information, absolute transparency, limitless choice, and more.

PRICING PANDEMONIUM

Pricing: more fluid and flexible than ever.

Customers have always been concerned with price, but thanks to a range of new technologies, services, and attitudes, their perceptions of price have become ever more complex. High or low (if not zero), fixed or fluid, universal or personal, businesses must respond by deploying price in ever more flexible ways.

The divisions between producers and consumers will continue to blur.

FUZZYNOMICS

New tools, platforms, and products are making the traditional divisions between consumers and producers increasingly fuzzy. Fueled by the desire for control, involvement, authenticity, self-expression, and/or relevance, the participation mega-trend will continue to grow as people jump into all aspects of the business arena, alongside—if not in the place of—brands.

REMAPPED

The epic power shifts in the global economy.

The rebalancing of the global economy, the great convergence, multipolar consumerism. Whatever you call it, the epic rise of emerging economies is not just expanding consumer markets—it's also creating new processes, practices, structures, business models, and brands that are remapping the business arena on a global scale.

POST-DEMOGRAPHIC

Time to throw out the old demographic models of consumer behavior.

People of all ages are shaking off conventions and constructing their own lifestyles and identities more freely than ever before. This will challenge organizations that still think in terms of consumption patterns that are defined by traditional demographic segments of age, gender, income, family status, and more.

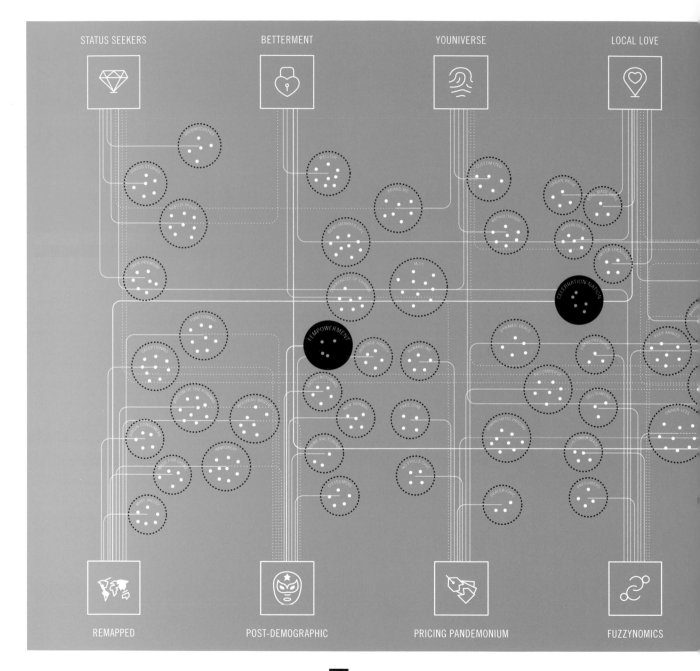

STATUS SEEKERS

BETTERMENT

YOUNIVERSE

LOCAL LOVE

REMAPPED

POST-DEMOGRAPHIC

PRICING PANDEMONIUM

FUZZYNOMICS

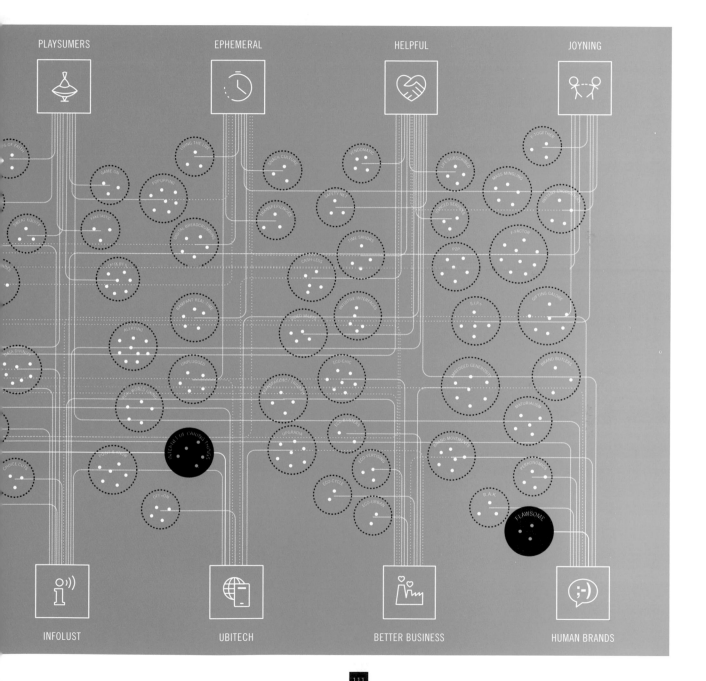

PLAYSUMERS

EPHEMERAL

HELPFUL

JOYNING

INFOLUST

UBITECH

BETTER BUSINESS

HUMAN BRANDS

A LIVING FRAMEWORK

Spotting trends as they emerge. Tracking trends as they evolve.

Too often, professional trend watchers imply there's some inherent gift they have that enables them to divine the future.

Now, we don't want to be the ones to spoil the party, but the reality is that with a solid Trend Framework and a little commitment, *any* switched-on business professional can spot and track trends, especially with the wealth of trend information now available to everyone at the tap of a finger (as outlined earlier in this chapter).

The best part of being a trend watcher? The more you do, the easier it gets! Once you have been scanning the business arena for some time, you should find that the vast majority of new innovations you see fit (at least fairly neatly) into the existing trends in your Trend Framework.

However, it's when new innovations *don't* fit naturally into the trends you have previously identified that things start to get interesting.

By this, we mean:

- When a new innovation that's exciting customers doesn't fit satisfactorily into any of your existing trends.
- When multiple examples repeatedly span the same 2-3 trends.
- When multiple examples of a trend start to point toward a new and specific direction.

These are all signals that you may be witnessing the emergence of a new trend, or the evolution of an existing trend.

The next stage is to question (either online or by asking your network of colleagues) whether

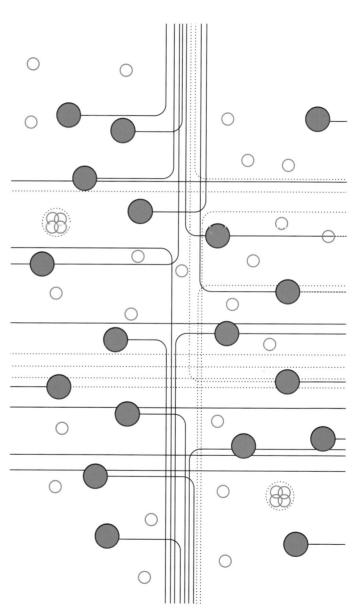

similar developments are occurring in other industries and/or markets. How are customers responding? Are similar signals visible across the four types of innovation (vision, business model, product/service, and marketing)? Is there quantitive data supporting and validating the direction of the trend?

As you start to gather more data points, you'll have a better idea of where customers—and their expectations—are headed, and ultimately where the opportunities for *you* might lie.

> NEXT

Having read this chapter, you now:

[1] Know how to add context and structure to your insights via a Trend Framework that takes in mega-trends, trends, and innovations;

[2] Understand the major forces shaping customer behavior and the business arena, and how we've captured them in our Trend Framework; and

[3] Understand how to develop and maintain your Trend Framework, and how to use it to spot new trends.

Indeed, having read the SCAN section of this book, you're well on the way to becoming a trend watcher! However, this is just the start of the trend journey.

....

Move on to the next section—FOCUS—to discover how to assess and prioritize the *right* trends for you.

....

FOCUS

WHAT TO RUN WITH, WHEN, AND HOW

[FOCUS]

Once you are spotting consumer trends, a
whole new set of questions becomes urgent.
Which trends offer your organization powerful
new innovation opportunities? And once
you've identified those trends, when and how
should you set about applying them?

These are some of the most fundamental
questions in the trend-driven innovation
process.

In this section, we'll see why most organizations
go about answering them the wrong way—and
learn how you can arrive at the right answers.

POST-DEMOGRAPHIC CONSUMERISM

A license to focus on surprising things.

Do you ever get the feeling that customer behaviors and mind-sets are becoming increasingly hard to predict? Becoming, in fact, chaotic?

Motorcycle brand Harley-Davidson—surely one of the world's most macho brands—sees 10,000 women a year attend its courses on how to ride and maintain a Harley. In Malaysia, 82 percent of 18-35s believe in preserving cultural connections through family values; only 57 percent of 37-60s believe the same. Meanwhile, 25 percent of U.S. mobile shoppers are over the age of 55.

RETHINKING FOCUS

This section is about singling out the trends that offer your organization the most powerful innovation opportunities.

Before we dive deeper into that, it will pay to address the underlying assumptions that guide your decisions on what to focus on, what to prioritize, and what to ignore. Because thanks to the profound shifts that we just glimpsed via those examples, in today's Expectation Economy many of those assumptions no longer

hold true. That means that many organizations end up focusing on the wrong things, and—what's more—missing rich new opportunities, too.

THE DEMISE OF DEMOGRAPHICS

So, why is it that leading innovators, marketers, and CEOs alike get it wrong when it comes to organizational focus?

Often, established ways of setting priorities have centered around the dividing lines that brands use to help map the consumer arena: industry, target market, and especially, customer demographics. Today, these categories can still play a meaningful role in setting focus. But only when your analysis of them is underpinned by an appreciation of the new fluidity of customer expectation that is the hallmark of the Expectation Economy.

That fluidity means that the model of customer behavior embodied by the traditional demographic segments—age, gender, income bracket, marital status, and many more—is fast losing its predictive power.

In this chapter, we'll see how the demise of the old, demographic-based model of customer behavior—and the rise of more complex, varied and, yes, chaotic modes and patterns of consumption—means brands must drop the old assumptions that anchored their focus, and instead embrace new priorities and new directions.

That means the trends that truly offer you the most powerful innovation opportunities might currently be those you assume are safe to ignore.

So let's get to work, and dive deeper into this new Post-Demographic Consumerism.

40%

overlap between the lists of 1,000 favorite music artists for 13-year-olds and 60-year-olds in the U.K.

32%

increase in the number of female video gamers over 50 between 2012 and 2013.

62%

of men in Asia disagree with the idea that "using grooming products is just a woman thing."

THROW OUT THE OLD ASSUMPTIONS—ABOUT YOUR BRAND AND CUSTOMERS—THAT UNDERPINNED YOUR FOCUS. IT'S TIME TO REFOCUS AROUND MORE FLUID, MORE COMPLEX CUSTOMER BEHAVIOR.

39%

of Chinese citizens in Tier II cities use social media, against 28% in Tier I cities.

49%

of over 65s use social media, up from 1% in 2006.

400%

increase in mixed-race marriages in the U.S. in the last 30 years.

A NEW DEMOGRAPHIC COMPLEXITY

For decades professionals have divided customers into demographic segments in order to better understand and predict their behavior. Think milliennials, the middle class, seniors, luxury customers, urbanites, and many more. And for decades, that shared language has served B2C industries (reasonably) well. You've almost certainly used it yourself when thinking about customers—and your entire organization's understanding of itself and its relationship to its customers may even be based around it.

But now, deep-running social, technological, and customer shifts mean that around the world people are no longer living the lives determined for them by their demographics. Liberated from traditional ideas about the lives they "should" live given their age, gender, income bracket, and more, these people are instead constructing lifestyles and identities of their own choosing.

You only have to glance at the consumer arena to see the evidence everywhere: customers simply aren't behaving as they "should" anymore. In the United States, a former WWE wrestler targets out-of-shape men with his DDP Yoga brand—and racks up $1 million in DVD sales in just six days after appearing on pitch-for-investment TV show *Shark Tank*. In Malaysia, the ancient and declining art of *wayung kulit* shadow puppetry is being reinvented using Star Wars characters, in shows proving popular with the young. In London, shoppers at high-end department store Selfridges use a straw to sip from miniature bottles of

Moët & Chandon sold to them from a vending machine, turning champagne into an on-the-go convenience.

We could go on (and on!).

The picture is complex, but at least in broad terms, the takeaway is simple. Organizations that continue to focus and set priorities via a reliance on old demographic certainties about the type of customer they serve will fall behind the expectations of their customers—and lose out on the chance to win entirely new customers, too.

Instead, the organizations that prosper will be those that are able to shake off old assumptions and accommodate the new Post-Demographic complexity. That means being open-minded—and, yes, daring—enough to focus on entirely new things.

And in order to do that, it will pay to know more about the four forces driving the rise of Post-Demographic Consumerism: access, permission, ability, and desire.

AROUND THE WORLD, CUSTOMERS ARE FREEING THEMSELVES FROM THE SHACKLES OF DEMOGRAPHIC DETERMINISM AND CONSTRUCTING LIFESTYLES AND IDENTITIES OF THEIR OWN CHOOSING.

WHY NOW

[1/4] ACCESS

From Boston to Beijing, customers
are amid a great convergence.

A SNAPSHOT . . .

In January 2015, Apple Senior VP of Marketing Phil Schiller tweeted that the company had sold its one billionth iOS device. Meanwhile, the international arm of Japanese clothes brand Uniqlo announced revenues of $2.8 billion in the six months leading up to February 2015; not a bad result for a brand whose popular cotton t-shirts sell for just under $13. With over 1,300 stores worldwide—including an 89,000-square-foot presence on Fifth Avenue—the brand said in a 2012 campaign, "Our clothes are made for all . . . going beyond age, gender, occupation, ethnicity, and all the other ways that define people." And while Facebook long ago relinquished its status as cool social network, it has cemented its identity as social utility, with 1.3 billion active monthly users as of December 2014.

. . . OF THE GLOBAL BRAIN

As never before, today's consumers move in a global space of shared information, ideas, culture, and brand familiarity.

The globalization of mass consumerism—and the borderless spread of online connectivity—means customers worldwide are building relationships with the same megabrands, from Apple, Uniqlo, and Facebook to Nike, IKEA, McDonald's, and many more. The result? A global universalization of taste, sensibility, and customer choice that respects no demographic boundaries and sees customers of all ages from Beijing to Boston having access to—and lusting after—the same smartphones, sneakers, and sushi.

126

[2/4] PERMISSION

The social norms that kept behavior predictable are fading away.

ONE STORY . . .

In August 2014, Turkish Deputy Prime Minister Bülent Arinc made a speech lamenting declining standards of behavior. Women, he advised, "should not laugh out loud in public." Across the coming days, thousands of Turkish women took to Twitter to post pictures of themselves defying Arinc and laughing out loud. Over 300,000 associated tweets were counted, many using the hashtag #direnkahkaha (resist laughter). Soon enough, a local campaign became a global one—and even British actress Emma Watson had posted a "laughing" Tweet. Of course, Turkey remains a relatively socially conservative society. But 2014's #direnkahkaha story points to a broader, and important, shift.

. . . MILLIONS OF NEW LIFESTYLES

Across many societies around the world, the old social norms that kept people tied to the lifestyles they "ought" to lead are in decline. Of course, that's not happening everywhere and not uniformly. But the broad direction of travel is clear: toward greater social liberalization. In 2001, the Netherlands became the first country to legalize gay marriage. By 2015, it was legal in 17 countries. The takeaway? These new social freedoms are allowing people to construct and display lifestyles of their choosing, rather than remain chained to the lifestyles dictated to them by their gender, age, and other demographic characteristics. And with that new freedom comes the freedom to *consume* as they choose, too.

[3/4] ABILITY

More choice means a more personal consumption.

CHOICE EXPLOSION . . .

If you're in any doubt over the near-stupefying level of choice available to customers in today's Expectation Economy, consider these three glimpses of the broader reality.

Customers who visit Nike's website to buy a pair of shoes can choose from a product range of over 1,000. The U.S. Environmental Protection Agency estimates there are more than 700 brands of bottled water sold in the United States alone. And it's estimated that there are 253 million different products for sale on Amazon.com, and those products are available to pretty much everyone: Amazon says its fulfillment centers deliver to over 180 countries.

. . . ALLOWS PERSONAL EXPRESSION

We're living through global explosion in product and service choice. Digital consumerism has not only made it easier than ever for customers to learn about, locate, and buy any product, it has also allowed them to experiment with new products at low (or zero) risk and cost, quickly discard anything that disappoints, and move on to the next experience. Thus empowered, these consumers are now more free than ever to consume more of what they want.

That means that today, not only do rising numbers have social permission to be the people they want, they are now more able than ever to express that individuality via their consumption: whether that's through the clothes they wear, the food they eat, the music they listen to, and more.

[4/4] DESIRE

Customers are seeking status in
new and less predictable ways.

CUSTOMER STATUS . . .

Between June and September 2014, over 17 million videos were shared on Facebook in which the subjects were drenched by a bucket of icy water. The #icebucketchallenge social media phenomenon started among ordinary users of the social network, but soon spread to celebrities and even politicians (Barack Obama quietly declined when nominated by Justin Bieber).

The challenge was in support of U.S. charity The ALS Foundation, for which it raised over $115 million. But behind the laudable intention to raise money for charity, even the most casual social commentator could discern another motive: the status that came with the implicit statement, "Look, I am a good person!"

. . . HAS DEMOCRATIZED

Pursuit of status is a primary motivator of almost all behavior. Traditionally, status meant wealth display: the flashy car or expensive watch. But new status symbols— experiences, authenticity, wellness, ethics—are more democratic, and, just like the #icebucketchallenge, more about "who I am" than "what I have." The result is to render customer behavior much less predictable by demographic means, as rich and poor, old and young all jockey for status. Indeed, in the Post-Demographic customer arena, where status does not have to cost money, the traditional status hierarchy is often reversed, as older, richer customers play catch-up to younger, less affluent, cooler counterparts.

POST-DEMOGRAPHIC BRAND STRATEGY

We saw in the previous section how the creation and spread of new customer expectations is the fuel that drives the Expectation Economy. Game-changing innovations create new expectations that customers then bring to bear on every experience, driving an endless cycle of ever-higher expectations.

EXPECTATION TRANSFER

Cast your mind back to that central insight about customer expectations—that they transfer between customers and across industry and other boundaries—and it becomes clear that the emergence of a Post-Demographic consumer arena is about expectation transfer, too. Post-Demographic Consumerism is really about saying that the world is now too complex, ideas too available, people too networked, and society too fluid for expectations to remain the preserve of any single demographic for long.

What does this mean for brands? Yes, young people—more experimental, less tied to existing commitments—will remain the most common early adopters. But now compelling innovations will be rapidly adopted by, and/or almost instantly reshape the expectations of, any and all demographics.

So, forget old thinking about the type of person who buys from your brand. But don't worry, that doesn't mean abandoning any attempt to focus. Rather, it means choosing to focus on trends that open your organization to customers you once assumed were "not for us."

These four key innovation opportunities can inform your navigation of the Post-Demographic world and your decisions about how and where to focus.

[1] **NEW NORMAL**

Across societies worldwide (though not uniformly), old social conventions are falling away. Brands should embrace the new, nontraditional lifestyles that are rising in their place.

[2] **HERITAGE HERESY**

In a world in which consumers are no longer behaving as expected, neither should brands. Be prepared to reimagine, subvert, or simply throw away decades of brand heritage and tradition and do something entirely unexpected.

[3] **CROSS-DEMOGRAPHIC FERTILIZATION**

Today, innovations cross demographic boundaries nearly instantly. So seek inspiration in demographics you've never looked at before.

[4] **HYPER-DEMOGRAPHIC TARGETING**

It's still possible to have a target customer in a Post-Demographic world. But instead of the old demographic segments, target narrower, self-created tribes of taste and interest.

SHIFTING YOUR FOCUS

[1/4] NEW NORMAL

Celebrate and cater to nontraditional lifestyles.

As old social norms fade away, behaviors and lifestyles that once had to remain hidden are allowed to bloom in full view, and altogether new ways of living are constructed. So how could a decision to embrace this New Normal—and cater to the new wants and needs it is creating—change how and where you focus?

Before answering, it pays to remember that the rise of the New Normal can look very different, depending on where you are. In the United States, it can mean rising acceptance of gay marriage: a February 2015 *Wall Street Journal* poll found 59 percent in favor. Meanwhile, in more socially conservative Asian societies it might mean changing attitudes to gender and relationships: in June 2014, China's Ministry of Civil Affairs said the divorce rate had jumped 13 percent in the preceding year.

So, does catering to the New Normal mean changing the tone of your marketing? Acknowledging and celebrating customer lifestyles you have previously ignored? Or both?

Let an awareness of the New Normal percolate into your discussions around focus and priority, and see where it takes you. Remember, the lifestyles of your customers—and potential customers—are changing; so should you.

[EXAMPLES]

COCA-COLA

CONTROVERSIAL MULTICULTURAL "AMERICA THE BEAUTIFUL" CAMPAIGN

Coca-Cola's 2014 Super Bowl ad featured "America the Beautiful" sung in a variety of languages (including Spanish, Hindi, and Hebrew) and by people from various ethnicities. The ad's celebration of multiculturalism caused controversy, which in turn caused others to defend Coke. Following the ad, U.S. 19- to 24-year-olds bought Coke products 20 percent more than in the preceding month.

BANCO DO BRASIL

MORTGAGES FOR SAME-SEX COUPLES

March 2013 saw Brazilian bank Banco do Brasil begin offering mortgages to same-sex couples. The lending scheme protects both partners and their children in the event of divorce, separation, or death. The initiative was supported by an ad campaign that showed a lesbian couple on their moving day alongside the slogan: "Mortgages for same-sex couples: at Bank of Brazil you can."

TANISHQ

INDIAN JEWELRY CELEBRATES NONTRADITIONAL FAMILIES

Indian jewelry brand Tanishq's recent campaigns have addressed shifting attitudes toward marriage. In 2013's "Tanishq Wedding Film," a bride is remarried in the presence of her daughter from a previous marriage. The video has over 1.1 million views on YouTube. Meanwhile, in a 2014 video, a grandmother advocates love-based marriage, challenging orthodoxy around arranged marriages.

[2/4]

HERITAGE HERESY

Play with, subvert, or even discard
your brand heritage.

Your brand heritage is a set of traditions aimed at speaking to the type of people who buy from you. But in a Post-Demographic world, people are no longer behaving to type, and that has profound implications for the relevance and usefulness of your brand.

The reality for many brands today is that the needs and wants of customers—who are constructing new, diverse, and more personally meaningful lifestyles—simply don't align with the narrative that brands have labored to build. For rising numbers of those customers, brand heritage and story have become at best irrelevant, and at worst an active barrier, one that prevents brands they might engage with from offering a product or service that's right for them, today. No wonder a recent survey found that the majority of people worldwide wouldn't care if 73 percent of brands disappeared tomorrow.

In a Post-Demographic world in which people are no longer behaving as they "should," neither will brands who want to keep up with existing customers and win over the entirely new ones waiting to engage. Instead, they'll commit brand heresies that see them make moves no one expected.

Want to commit a heresy of your own? Start by asking: "What should our brand never do?"

[EXAMPLES]

HARLEY-DAVIDSON

50 MILLION TREES BY 2020

For decades, motorcycle brand Harley-Davidson has traded on its rebel image. But October 2014 saw the brand make an altogether different move: it partnered with charity The Nature Conservancy on a pledge to plant 50 million trees worldwide by 2020. The brand committed $550,000 in annual grants and pledged to tap its global biking community for support.

MOËT HENNESSY

INDIAN SPARKLING WINES

The Moët brand is synonymous with champagne—and with France. But October 2013 saw LVMH-owned Moët Hennessy take a radical departure by launching two varieties of sparkling wine in Mumbai. The Chandon Brut and Chandon Rosé Brut wines are made at vineyards in the Nashik region of India. They are priced at around $20, against around $80 for Moët & Chandon's Brut Imperial.

VERSACE

COUNTERFEITS INSPIRE COLLECTION

Italian fashion house Versace has always traded on a sense of Italian style and on the rarefied design sensibilities typical of any high-fashion house. But in October 2013 the brand subverted these key principles by partnering with British-Sri Lankan recording artist M.I.A. to launch the M.I.A. x Versace Versus Collection, a line that takes inspiration from the Versace counterfeits found in many markets.

[3/4]

CROSS-DEMOGRAPHIC FERTILIZATION

Be inspired by—and cater to—entirely new demographics.

In the Post-Demographic arena, your customers, and people who are not yet your customers, aren't waiting for your permission to live the lives they want. Seniors are participating in the Collaborative Economy. Young people are cherishing and interpreting old customs in new ways. Affluent consumers are prioritizing value, and those with few resources are seeking a taste of luxury.

Today, the most compelling innovations move across demographic boundaries nearly instantly, as all demographic groups become free to seek out the new products, services, and experiences that speak most powerfully to them. One way to keep up? Shift your focus to traditional demographic groups you've never considered before, both as a source of inspiration and as target customers.

Are seniors your conventional target? What compelling new innovations are millennials embracing that could help inspire a new product? Always targeted women? How could you tweak your offering to turn it into something compelling for men?

The variations are endless, but the key message is simple: consumers aren't respecting demographic boundaries anymore, so neither should you.

[EXAMPLES]

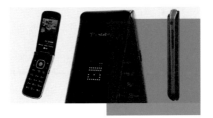

LULULEMON

YOGA STORE FOR MEN

In November 2014 Canada-based yoga wear brand lululemon—long associated with stylish women's yoga clothing—opened a New York store aimed at men. The 1,600-square-foot space caters to male yogis and features a section called The Joinery where shorts are custom made. Lululemon's menswear sales were around $216 million in 2013. The brand is targeting $1 billion "across the next few years," says CEO Laurent Potdevin.

LG

SMARTPHONE FOR SENIORS

In September 2014, LG launched the LG Wine Smart cellphone in Korea: a flip phone that doubles as an Android smartphone. Designed for the elderly, the handset features a large keypad button and dedicated instant messaging button, alongside a "safe keeper" function that alerts friends or family if the user falls.

THUG KITCHEN

"GANGSTER" VEGAN DIET ADVICE

Traditionally, vegan cookbooks take aim at an affluent, aspirational demographic via an earnest and even (pseudo)-spiritual tone of voice. By contrast, the Thug Kitchen cookbook—an offshoot of the blog of the same name—aims to win over an altogether different set of customers via a promise to "abuse you into a healthier diet." Liberal use of profanity and humor is combined with advice on healthy eating on a budget.

[4/4]

HYPER-DEMOGRAPHIC TARGETING

Target niche tribes of taste and interest.

This chapter is all about the waning power of the traditional demographic model of customer segmentation. The irony here is that demographics are as relevant as ever today. But the nature of those useful demographic groups has radically changed. Rather than setting their sights on the traditional, broad segments, smart brands will target narrower demographic tribes of shared taste, interest, and sensibility.

Psychographics—close study of customer lifestyles, interests, attitudes, and more—is nothing new. And of course, it's received wisdom now that the Internet has made it possible to identify and cater to "the long tail:" small tribes with a shared but niche interest.

But today, the oceans of data that customers are creating via their online searches, smartphone use, and more are making entirely new kinds of data-driven targeting possible. Now, customers needn't actively cluster into self-selected tribes—or even consciously know they are a member of a tribe—for your brand to reach out to them. Rather, each customer is constantly expressing their tastes, interests, values, and habits via the data they spin off as they go about daily life.

Today, brands that want to target customers effectively will use that data to shape new products and marketing around the real lifestyles and mind-sets of customers, rather than around the demographic assumptions of the past.

[EXAMPLES]

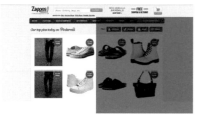

ZAPPOS

PINTEREST RECOMMENDATIONS

August 2012 saw U.S.-based e-tailer Zappos launch PinPointing, a service that makes product recommendations based on Pinterest boards and pins. Users can enter the name of any Pinterest user and see apparel, accessories, and footwear recommendations that are based on the type of images pinned. Shoppers can click through to purchase items on Zappos.

BARCLAYCARD

SPENDING HABITS TRIGGER DEALS

In May 2013, Barclaycard launched Bespoke Offers, a tailored deals brand that offers U.K. customers relevant prepaid deals and discounts based on their preferences and previous spending habits. Deals can be accessed through personalized daily emails or via a dedicated smartphone app, and can be purchased using Barclaycard's bPay payment system.

UNILEVER

DATA-DRIVEN HAIR TUTORIALS

December 2013 saw Unilever partner with Google to launch its All Things Hair YouTube channel, in partnership with a number of popular British YouTube vloggers. The brand commissions the vloggers to create short shows based on real-time search data, ensuring that the content is relevant. The channel was viewed over 13 million times in its first year, and Unilever expanded the initiative to Canada.

POST-DEMOGRAPHIC PRIORITIES

There is no formal methodology when it comes to how to use your awareness of Post-Demographic Consumerism as you identify and prioritize the trends that are important to you. The move toward a Post-Demographic world is itself too complex and too fluid to be captured by any such scheme.

Instead, you should let an awareness of the shifts outlined in this chapter percolate through the thinking and discussions you have as you set about identifying the trends you want to run with, and prioritizing their application.

To help you in this process, here are some Post-Demographic questions to ask:

[1] **New Normal**: how can we celebrate and cater to non-traditional lifestyles and identities?

[2] **Heritage Heresy**: what should our brand *never* do? What would it look like if we did just that?

[3] **Cross-Demographic Fertilization**: what entirely new demographic groups can we take inspiration from and cater to?

[4] **Hyper-Demographic Targeting**: what new tribes of shared taste and interest could we target?

WHEN SETTING YOUR FOCUS,
REMEMBER: CONSUMERS ARE
EMBRACING NEW BEHAVIORS.
SO SHOULD YOU.

> **NEXT**

Having read this chapter, you now:

[1]   Understand the profound shift in the consumer arena that is the rise of Post-Demographic Consumerism;

[2]   See how this shift poses a challenge to the thinking most organizations have traditionally used when they focus and set priorities; and

[3]   Know the four key opportunities that can help you navigate this new, more fluid customer arena.

....

Next, let's drill deeper into the process of choosing the trends you'll run with by learning a key secret: almost any trend can offer you powerful innovation opportunities.

....

EVALUATING TRENDS FOR OPPORTUNITY

Why almost any trend can offer you powerful opportunity.

You've read SCAN and you're spotting trends. Maybe you're spotting more than you can handle! But how can you isolate that crucial handful of trends that will see you launch a killer new product or service, create a campaign that gets everyone talking, innovate your way to a new business model, or even overhaul your entire vision of your organization?

In this chapter, we'll examine a core truth when it comes to consumer trends, one you've already glimpsed via the three core elements of a trend and the previous chapter on Post-Demographic Consumerism. That is, almost any trend can offer you powerful innovation opportunities; unlocking those opportunities is all about adapting the trend for your context.

To see how, we'll look at the three key dimensions of adaptation that you can use to do just that: trend maturity, industry, and locality.

Evaluating a trend against those three dimensions will allow you to see deeper into the innovation opportunities that a given trend offers you. And what you learn from that evaluation will prove invaluable when you come to prioritize the trends you're going to work with, which you'll be doing in 3.3 using the Consumer Trend Radar.

So let's get started, and learn more about why identifying the opportunities offered by trends is all about adaptation.

TREND ADAPTATION

Trends are (nearly) universal. So it's all about adaptation.

In September 2013, Lego unveiled Professor C Bodin: its first female scientist character. March 2014 saw Brazilian bank Itaú Unibanco launch Mulher Empreendedora (Woman Entrepreneur), an initiative aimed at female entrepreneurs that includes networking events and seminars. Meanwhile, in July 2014, U.S. retailer Walmart launched its Women Owned initiative, which sees it sell a range of products produced by women entrepreneurs.

Walmart, Itaú Unibanco, and Lego: three brands with little in common. But all three have rolled out successful applications of the FEMPOWERMENT trend that we first saw in SCAN (in Chapter 2.3), which is seeing brands empowering women to think and acts beyond gender stereotypes.

The idea that your organization can apply almost any trend successfully might seem strange. But it's a direct consequence of the nature of both trends—more specifically, their universality—and the global consumer arena.

TRENDS ARE UNIVERSAL

In SCAN, we looked at the three fundamental elements of any trend: basic needs, drivers of change, and innovations.

Re-looking at basic needs and drivers of change can help you understand how consumer trends are essentially universal in their nature.

[1] **Basic needs**: these fundamental human needs and wants—connection, security, excitement, and so on—are universal to all people.

[2] **Drivers of change**: from the global embrace of smartphone culture to social liberalization across many societies worldwide, in an increasingly globalized world the external changes driving a trend are almost always playing out somehow in any region.

So, trends themselves are increasingly universal and global, with the basic needs and drivers of change that inform them almost always playing themselves out *somehow* in any given context. As a result you can take almost any trend, and it's less a matter of *whether* it is relevant to a given industry or locality, and more a question of *how* it is relevant.

THREE AXES OF ADAPTATION

At heart, intelligent adaptation of a trend means asking a key question: how are the new customer expectations that inform this trend playing out in *my* context?

In this chapter, we'll take a closer look at how to answer that question by evaluating a trend against three key axes of adaptation: trend maturity, locality, and industry. Evaluating a trend against the three axes is the key to drilling deeper into the opportunities that the trend offers you.

And if you're already wondering, "If every trend offers me powerful opportunities, how will I ever choose which to apply?" then don't worry. As we'll see in the next chapter, that depends above all on *you*—your aims, capabilities, and resources. But first, let's get started on a closer look at the three axes of trend adaptation.

[1] TREND MATURITY

Am I too late? Am I too early?

August 2012 saw Tinder launch a dating app into a crowded market, riding a trend for digital-fueled social connection that's been running for well over a decade. Meanwhile Oculus Rift raised $2.4 million on Kickstarter, tapping into a trend for virtual reality that is still in its infancy, and has yet to touch the lives of most customers.

"Am I too early to this trend?" "Am I too late?" Those are two of the most common questions we hear from clients practicing trend-led innovation. Here's what we tell them in a nutshell: stop worrying about too early and too late, and focus on great adaptation for today.

Across the next few pages, we'll look at why that holds true.

First, we'll examine how customer adoption of new innovations in the Expectation Economy has become fluid and unpredictable.

Next, via case studies of Tinder and Seventh Generation, we'll see how it's great adaptation of a trend for the needs and wants of today's customers that counts.

Last, we'll look at *how* to adapt any trend for today by evaluating the trend's three fundamental elements. And we'll see how innovators have done just that with the pop-up trend across the last 13 years.

The purpose of all this? Learn how to evaluate a trend against today's context, and you'll be able to drill deeper into the opportunities that trend offers you—and to decide whether you want to pursue them.

The challenge to being ahead of the trend . . . is finding out how does the problem you're solving touch customers' lives. If you are a good systems thinker you can almost always find a point at which that problem connects with something that they care about.

Jeffrey Hollender

EVALUATING TRENDS FOR OPPORTUNITY
[1] TREND MATURITY

Big Bang Disruption
Adoption Curve

FORGET TOO EARLY
AND TOO LATE

While too late and too early are among the most common concerns we hear from people when it comes to trends, they are concerns of decreasing relevance in today's Expectation Economy.

The pace of change is too relentless and customer adoption of the new too fluid for "too early" and "too late" to be meaningful in the way they once were. Instead, unpredictable patterns of adoption are the norm—and great adaptation of trends for *today* is the answer.

TRADITIONAL ADOPTION

In his famous 1962 book *The Diffusion of Innovations*, Everett Rogers established the traditional theoretical model of how innovations—new ideas, technologies, products, and more—are adopted by both individuals and groups. Rogers said that the adoption of an innovation predictably follows a bell curve, starting with innovators, then early adopters (Rogers coined the phrase), going through the majority, and ending with laggards.

ADOPTION DISRUPTED

Today, thanks to forces driving the emergence of a Post-Demographic customer arena—instant access to information, the decline of traditional social norms, the diversification of status seeking and more—adoption patterns have become much less stable.

Sometimes, adoption by the global mainstream can happen almost instantly (see the excellent *Big Bang Disruption* by Larry Downes and Paul Nunes for more on this). In 2015, for example, WhatsApp

Traditional Consumer
Adoption Curve

boasted 700 million monthly active users: a user base assembled in just six years.

At other times, adoption can suddenly hit a tipping point, as the case study on Tinder on the next page shows. But of course, a world of instant adoption can also be one of instant disengagement, too. Remember Draw Something? Back in 2012 the app gained 35 million downloads in six weeks, only for the user base to plummet by millions within weeks of being acquired by mobile games giant Zynga, as people moved on to the next hot mobile game.

The underlying lesson? In the Expectation Economy, the bell curve model of customer adoption is no longer a reliable guide. And that means innovators should—within reasonable limits, of course—drop notions of "too early" and "too late" and focus on great adaptation for *now*.

Let's see how the innovators behind Tinder did just that.

IN THE EXPECTATION ECONOMY, ADOPTION OF NEW PRODUCTS AND SERVICES IS FLUID AND UNPREDICTABLE. SO FORGET TOO EARLY AND TOO LATE, AND ADAPT FOR TODAY!

[FEATURE]
TINDER

The ultra-successful dating app is a case study in the power of adaptating an established trend.

By mid-2014, Tinder was boasting 1 billion swipes a day (revisit Chapter 2.1 for more details on the popular dating app).

But when the app launched in August 2012, there were already several other successful mobile dating apps in the market, including OKCupid's, which had around 60 percent market share (see the graph opposite). The innovators behind Tinder might well have concluded: "We're too late to the trend for digital-fueled romantic connections."

Instead, they adapted that trend for the time. That meant creating a service that was thoroughly mobile first, serving social connections that were ultra-location specific and near-instant. It meant integration with Facebook to dispense with a lengthy "tell us about you" signup. And it meant nailing expectations of protection from unwanted advances by ensuring users can't contact one another unless they signal mutual interest.

Still, for around a year, adoption was slow. But in the middle of

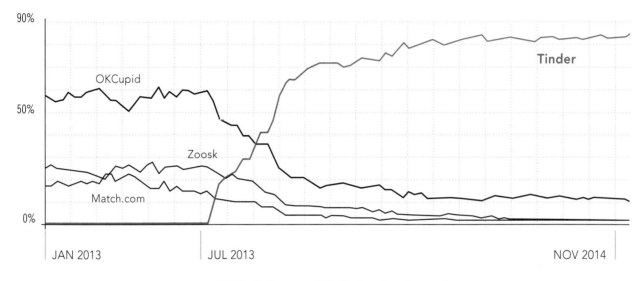

Mobile dating apps. U.S. Market share by session.

2013, the app hit a tipping point fueled by marketing on U.S. college campuses and great word of mouth. Within months Tinder had blown the incumbents away and has rarely dropped out of the most downloaded apps since then.

This example of the unpredictable, accelerated adoption possible in today's Expectation Economy is a case study in how notions of "too early" and "too late" just don't hold true. Instead, as the innovators behind Tinder intuitively understood, applying a trend now means adapting it around the human nature, external change, and new expectations as they are currently manifesting themselves.

SEVENTH GENERATION

The company jumped early on the trend for a more conscious consumerism—and adapted it well.

Entrepreneur Jeffrey Hollender co-founded sustainable personal care and household product company Seventh Generation in 1989, well before many people were aware of the impact of their consumption. He explains how one can overcome being early to a trend:

"What interests me is the role businesses can play in creating trends—and I'm particularly interested in trends that influence society in a positive way. Most people think of trends as things that need to be followed rather than created; but imagine how different the world would be if all businesses were creating healthy, responsible consumer trends, rather than focusing on providing superficial benefits to customers at a very high cost to society and the environment.

"So I'm never interested in waiting. The challenge to being ahead of the trend—which I have been for most of my life—is to find a way to start a dialogue with the consumer. Perhaps you want to provide a solution to a problem they don't

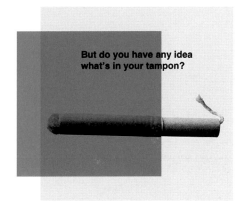

But do you have any idea what's in your tampon?

yet know exists. So you need to ask: how does this problem touch their lives and what they care about? Solving that problem can be difficult, time-consuming, and expensive—but I would never want to be limited by what people think is currently 'on trend.'

"Take our organic cotton tampons as an example. Around 15 years ago, we bought a company named Organic Essentials with a focus on growing cotton organically because of the damage that pesticides were doing to the environment and farm workers.

"Because consumers were not aware of the fact that the cotton in tampons contained pesticide residue as well as dioxin left over from the bleaching process, these issues didn't really connect with consumers. But if you change the angle and ask how much pesticide residue is in the tampon that a customer is using, and what harm could that be doing—thus taking the same issue, but emphasizing a different part of the system—that problem clearly becomes more much compelling.

"The organic cotton tampons launched in 2008 and we quickly got good distribution. Today, feminine care is a $5- to $10-million-a-year business for the company."

Organic cotton tampons are just one of the many forward-thinking sustainable products that have helped propel Seventh Generation to over $300 million a year in annual sales by 2014 (although Hollender left Seventh Generation in 2010).

ADAPT ANY TREND FOR MATURITY

Where does this leave you? We've seen how customer adoption in the Expectation Economy can be unpredictable. And we've looked at the answer to that for trend-led innovators: don't worry about too early and too late; instead, adapt your trend for today.

The good news? Adapting a trend for today doesn't have to be a mysterious, intuition-led process. Instead, it's about evaluating the three core elements of the trend and how they are coming together to create new expectations.

[1] **Basic needs**: how are the basic needs that underlie this trend being expressed now? If the trend is an established one, how has this changed over time?

[2] **Drivers of change**: how has the external change driving this trend evolved? What have those changes meant for your customers?

[3] **Innovations**: what underlying insights can you draw from the examples of the trends you're seeing now, both into how the trend is playing out in customers' lives and how that will develop?

Analyze the three fundamental elements of any trend, and you'll be primed to answer the key question: how are the customer expectations that inform this trend playing out now?

....

Adapting a trend for today doesn't have to be a mysterious process. It's about evaluating the three core elements of the trend and how they are coming together to create new expectations.

....

[CASE STUDY]
ADAPTATION IN ACTION: POP-UPS

We first flagged pop-ups way back in 2004, when we highlighted the trend for temporary retail spaces that offer customers a sense of surprise and urgency, and the chance to live an experience that most other shoppers won't have.

Of course, since 2004 the trend has spread worldwide, been deployed by countless brands, and become a standard part of the retail playbook. And as you'll see in the trend timeline overleaf, across the years the trend has evolved from standard retail plays, to tech-fueled and experiential pop-ups, toward today's pop-ups that offer more lasting and meaningful social value.

Let's analyze the pop-up trend via the three fundamental elements:

[1] **Basic needs**: the desire for excitement, surprise, and memorable experiences that underlie this trend is ageless.

[2] **Drivers of change**: from more ubiquitous online retail, to growth in the status value of rare experiences, to globalization and the simultaneous rising importance of the local, since 2003 the external changes driving this trend have undergone huge evolution.

[3] **Innovations**: constant innovation when it comes to pop-ups has both served and set new expectations for the trend (see timeline overleaf).

The result? Across the years these external changes have acted to create new expectations of digital-style convenience and participation, of exciting and status-worthy experiences, of brands that deliver real and lasting social value to localities, and more.

[THE EVOLUTION OF]

POP-UPS

One trend adapted for today—over, and over, and over.

[DEFINITION]

Temporary retail spaces that offer one-off experiences of shopping in new places and in new ways.

2002

PURE RETAIL POP-UP

TARGET

POP-UP ON THE HUDSON RIVER

Tapping into a rising trend for ephemeral retail spaces, and to test the Manhattan market, clothes retailer Target opened a temporary, floating store on the Hudson River. Housed in a barge, the pop-up showcased Christmas holiday merchandise.

2006

LOCAL EVENT LINKED POP-UP

NIKE

POP-UP WHEN LEBRON PLAYS IN NYC

Taking aim at customer demand for local relevance, Nike tied a SoHo pop-up to a local event. The brand marked a clash between the Cleveland Cavaliers and the New York Knicks by opening a six-day pop-up selling limited-edition Zoom LeBron IV NYC trainers. A queue of over 100 gathered outside the store before opening.

2011
SOCIALLY CONSCIOUS POP-UP

H&M

GLOBAL WATER CHARITY POP-UP
Swedish clothing retailer H&M
launched a pop-up store in The
Hague's popular Scheveningen
resort intended to tap into rising
customer expectations of a more
ethical consumption. A variety of
essentials were available at the
shipping container-style shop
on the beach, and 25 percent of
proceeds went to global charity
WaterAid.

2013
TECH-FUELED, MAKER POP-UP

YRSTORE

DESIGN AND PRINT OWN T-SHIRTS
YrStore was a pop-up store
in London where customers
could satisfy their burgeoning
expectations of tech-fueled
participation and creativity. Via
a touchscreen system, shoppers
designed their own t-shirts with
either stock images or their own
artwork. Finalized designs could be
printed immediately in-store.

2015
ART EXHIBITION OR POP-UP?

TARGET

ART INSTALLATION MEETS POP-UP
In March 2015—and 13 years
after its pop-up on the Hudson
River—Target opens the Target
Too exhibition space in NYC.
Visitors found 12 murals, displays,
and sculptures based on Target
products and could download an
app to discover augmented reality
features of the exhibition and
purchase the products on which the
installations were based.

[2] LOCALITY

What opportunities does this trend offer me in my target market?

Often, you'll identify consumer trends by spotting clusters of innovations from outside the market—continent, country, city, neighborhood—you are targeting.

But with proper adaptation you can extract powerful innovation opportunities for your target market(s).

Of course, there are exceptions to that general rule. In the rare cases in which the drivers of change that inform the trend are absent from the market in question, you've found a trend that can't (yet) be applied in this locality. For example, clearly the INTERNET OF CARING THINGS trend (see Chapter 2.3) cannot be applied in the ever-dwindling number of places with no Internet connectivity (but read about the Lumkani fire detector, coming up, to be reminded of how innovative technologies *can* serve the basic need for safety among populations without Internet).

For all other cases, evaluating the trend against your local context will allow you to drill deeper into the nature of the opportunities it offers. And that means taking a close look at how the basic needs, drivers of change, and innovations are coming together to create new expectations in that locality.

CASE STUDY: SAFETY NET

Some years ago, we started to spot an increasing number of digital tools and services intended to help keep users safe. That led us to identify the SAFETY NET trend, and since then we've seen it adapted by innovators around the world to suit local context (you can see five examples of this in the next few pages).

So, how would you evaluate the SAFETY NET trend against your local context?

Again, it's a case of looking closely at how the three fundamental elements of the trend are playing out:

[1] **Basic needs**: clearly the key aspect of human nature that underlies this trend is the desire to stay safe. What is specific about the way it's manifesting in your locality? One example: in China ineffective regulations and unreliable information make environmental and food safety a key concern. Meanwhile, in the United States and Western Europe data privacy has recently become a higher priority for many citizens in the wake of revelations about intelligence agency surveillance.

[2] **Drivers of change**: the key driving change here is digital technology. How is this playing out in your target market? What is smartphone penetration? Is use of the Internet clustered around certain target customers or more evenly spread?

[3] **Innovations**: how are examples of the SAFETY NET trend serving and creating new customer expectations? What underlying lessons can I draw for my locality?

Answer those questions, and you'll be primed to answer the key question when it comes to local adaptation: "How are the customer expectations informing this trend—in this case the expectation that new digital technologies will be put in the service of personal safety and risk reduction—playing out in my locality?"

[THE LOCALITY OF]

SAFETY NET

Five innovations. Five
adaptations for local
context.

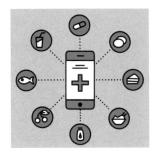

INDIA
PERSONAL SAFETY OF WOMEN

[DEFINITION]
New digital technologies
and services—apps,
platforms, devices, and
more—to avoid or react
to danger and minimize
personal risk.

HIMMAT
POLICE SAFETY APP FOR WOMEN
The safety of women has been
a key issue in India since the
gang rape of a student in Delhi
in December 2012 and the
nationwide outcry that followed. In
January 2015 Delhi Police launched
the Himmat app. Targeted at
women, the app allows a user
to shake her phone to send an
emergency alert to police and an
SMS to two selected contacts.

CHINA
FOOD SAFETY

CHINA SURVIVAL GUIDE
APP PROVIDES FOOD SAFETY INFO
Food safety scandals—including
the infamous 2011 discovery of a
stockpile of milk powder tainted
with melamine—are a fact of life in
China. Available from May 2012,
the China Survival Guide is a free
app that offers information on
food safety. The app is regularly
updated, with data organized into
12 categories, including beverages
and dairy.

U.S. AND EUROPE

DATA PROTECTION

MERCEDES-BENZ

CLOUD PROTECTS DRIVER DATA

June 2013 revelations on U.S. government surveillance made data privacy a key concern for many citizens across the United States and Europe. September 2014 saw Mercedes-Benz announce a cloud-computing system designed to protect driver data. Users can control how much of their driving data is viewable by others and erase all data once they have completed a journey.

SOUTH AFRICA

SLUM FIRES

LUMKANI

FIRE DETECTOR FOR SLUM DWELLERS

In January 2013, a series of fires hit two Cape Town townships, leaving 4,000 homeless. Launched in 2013, Lumkani is a low-cost smart fire detector for slum dwellers. Innovative heat-sensing technology can distinguish between cooking and a dangerous fire. If a fire is detected by one device, all the others in a 100-meter radius will also sound an alarm.

BRAZIL

CHILD ABUSE

PROTEJA BRASIL

ANONYMOUS REPORTING APP

UNICEF estimates that around 3 million children in Brazil are victims of child labor. Available from November 2013, mobile app Proteja Brasil allows Brazilians to send anonymous reports of child labor or other forms of child abuse. The free app was developed by UNICEF in partnership with Secretaria de Direitos Humanos and Ilhasoft Mobile.

[3] INDUSTRY

What opportunities does this trend offer me in my industry?

What happens if you spot a cluster of innovations in a particular industry—not your own—that point toward a newly emerging trend? Just as nearly any trend can be adapted for maturity and locality, so can nearly any trend be adapted for your industry, too.

Of course, there will be exceptions that hang on the nature of your industry. To take an extreme example, it's unlikely that a trend built around the need for thrills and a sense of danger could be successfully adapted by an airline.

But in almost all cases adaptation for your industry will be possible. And drilling down into the opportunities offered by the trend means evaluating it against your industry context.

BRAND MOVEMENTS

Across the last few years, rising numbers of brands from diverse industries have innovated around a trend we call BRAND MOVEMENTS, by launching campaigns and taking action to create positive change in the world: social, environmental, and more. So

how would you set about adapting this trend for your industry?

Let's go back to the three core elements of any trend:

[1] **Basic needs**: the key aspect of human nature underlying this trend is to be a good person—and feel good about oneself—by living (and consuming) according to a vision of what is right. That's a universal human impulse that will be relevant whatever industry you're in.

[2] **Drivers of change**: many changes are helping drive this trend, but principal among them is

rising awareness of environmental, social, and other problems and the role brands can play in them. So how is this awareness playing out differently across industries? For example, in the beauty industry rising numbers of customers are troubled by the negative impacts on girls and women of unrealistic standards of beauty. Meanwhile, in the energy industry, rising numbers of customers are concerned about damage to the environment.

[3] **Innovations**: how are examples of this trend across industries

both serving and setting customer expectation? What underlying lessons can I draw from examples outside my industry?

Answer these questions, and you'll be able to see how the core elements of this trend are coming together to create new customer expectations in your industry. Yes, the central new expectation informing this trend is that brands will take action to drive positive change. But how will this expectation be brought to bear on your industry, and how can you best

serve it? A physical space? A digital service? A campaign?

Overleaf, we look at how five brands, each from a different industry, answered those questions to generate their own BRAND MOVEMENT.

[THE ADAPTATION OF]

BRAND MOVEMENTS

One trend. Five industries.

[DEFINITION]

Brands are running campaigns—and taking action—to generate positive change in the world around them.

FOOD
GANG CULTURE

KENCO
SUPPORT AND TRAINING FOR HONDURAN YOUNGSTERS

U.K. coffee brand Kenco is owned by Mondelez International, the single largest purchaser of coffee beans from Honduras. In August 2014, Kenco revealed details of its year-long Coffee vs Gangs initiative. The U.K.-based coffee brand gave 20 young people in violent areas of Honduras training and support to build careers as coffee farmers.

PERSONAL CARE
SOCIAL TABOOS

WHISPER
CAMPAIGN CHALLENGES SOCIAL TABOO IN INDIA

An Indian superstition holds that menstruating women should not touch a pickle jar because they will contaminate the pickles. June 2014 saw feminine hygiene brand Whisper launch the #TouchThePickle campaign, encouraging women to earn vouchers by speaking out against outdated social norms.

FINANCIAL
CIVIC REGENERATION

JPMORGAN CHASE & CO
$100 MILLION AND STAFF EXPERTISE
FOR CITY OF DETROIT

In 2013, the city of Detroit filed
for bankruptcy, with $18 billion
in debts. June 2014 saw bank
JPMorgan Chase commit $100
million to help regenerate the
city. The bank also established the
Detroit Service Corps, which sees
top-performing employees deliver
advice to local nonprofits.

SPORTS
RACISM

BOTAFOGO
BRAZILIAN SOCCER TEAM TAKES
STANCE AGAINST RACISM

April 2014 saw Brazilian soccer
team Botafogo and sponsor Puma
unveil a kit with inverted black and
white stripes. Part of a campaign
against racism in soccer, the shirt
was meant to show that black
and white are interchangeable.
Via a dedicated microsite fans
could create images of themselves
wearing the new shirt.

BEVERAGES
LGBT RIGHTS

BREWDOG
ANTI-PUTIN BEER TO SUPPORT LGBT
RIGHTS

In 2013, Russia passed a law against
gay "propaganda" that was widely
seen as an attack on LGBT rights.
Ahead of the 2014 Winter Olympics
in Sochi, irreverent Scottish craft
beer brand BrewDog unveiled a
beer called "Hello My Name Is
Vladimir." BrewDog donated 50
percent of profits to charities that
help oppressed minorities.

ALWAYS BE EVALUATING

Keep the three axes in mind whenever you spot a trend.

In this chapter, we've looked more closely at how any trend can offer you powerful innovation opportunities. And, crucially, we've also seen how to drill down deeper into the nature of those opportunities by evaluating a trend against three axes of adaptation:

[1] **Trend maturity**: how are the customer expectations that inform this trend playing out now?

[2] **Locality**: how are the customer expectations that inform this trend playing out in my target locality?

[3] **Industry**: how are the customer expectations that inform this trend playing out in my industry?

Make it a habit to keep these three questions in mind whenever you spot a trend. And remember, the answers will change over time, so it pays to constantly evaluate and reevaluate the trends you're tracking.

Doing so will help you see how a trend is evolving over time and inside your target market and industry.

And as we've seen, it will ensure you have a clear picture of the innovation opportunities that a trend offers. And that will guide your thinking when you come to select and prioritize the trends that are most important to you—a process that is the subject of the next chapter.

WHENEVER YOU SPOT A
TREND, KEEP IN MIND
THE THREE AXES OF
ADAPTATION: MATURITY,
LOCALITY, INDUSTRY.

> NEXT

Having read this chapter, you now:

[1] Understand why almost *any* trend can offer your
     organization powerful innovation opportunities; and

[2] Have seen how to evaluate a trend against the three
     axes of adaptation: trend maturity, locality, and
     industry.

....

Armed with that and an understanding of Post-
Demographic Consumerism, it's time to start prioritizing
the trends that you will work with. That's the subject of
the next chapter—and the Consumer Trend Radar.

....

[FOCUS]

THE CONSUMER TREND RADAR

Create a visual, shareable plan of your trend-led strategy.

In the last chapter, you saw how almost any trend can offer you powerful opportunities. And how evaluating a trend against three dimensions of external context—trend maturity, industry, and locality—can help you frame the nature of those opportunities.

But the FOCUS process is far from over. Sure, your trend evaluations will already be pointing you toward the handful of trends—a typical range is between 3 and 10—that look most interesting to you. But how can you take those trends and create a concrete, actionable plan on which ones you will commit to running with, when, and how?

The answers to those questions depend on you. More specifically, on your organization's goals and priorities, its capabilities and resources, and the vision your team has of your shared future.

To create your plan, you must ask:

- Which trends should we apply now, and which later?
- What area(s) of our business or our offering should these trends impact on?

- How many resources should we commit to our application of this trend?

The Consumer Trend Radar (CTR) is a powerful tool that facilitates this assessment. The result is a single sheet of paper containing a shareable visualization of your trend-led strategy.

In this chapter, we'll walk you through using the CTR step-by-step, including a look at some worked examples.

INTRODUCING THE CTR

A summary of this tool and planning a session around it.

 Head online to download a poster size CTR template.

WHEN TO USE

For businesses and nonprofits: the CTR can form the basis of a powerful annual or quarterly trend-led strategy planning session. That session could address your entire organization or be specific to a department or team within your organization.

For agencies and consultancies: use the CTR to identify and plan the application of trends that are important to a new client. Take your completed radar with you to your next client presentation!

PLANNING A RADAR SESSION

The radar can be used by an individual or a team. But wherever possible choose the latter, because collective discussion around the CTR is likely to expose a range of different underlying assumptions about the functions, capabilities, outputs, and values of your organization.

During the session you'll be called upon to assess each trend against three dimensions—Innovation Target, Priority, and Response—positioning each trend on the CTR accordingly (a detailed How To Use guide is available later in this chapter).

The end result will be a one-page, visual map of your trend-led strategy, which tells you which trends you're going to apply, when, and how.

To run this session, you need nothing more than a large, blank CTR, Post-it notes, and pens. But a large pot of coffee certainly won't hurt, either.

THE CONSUMER TREND RADAR

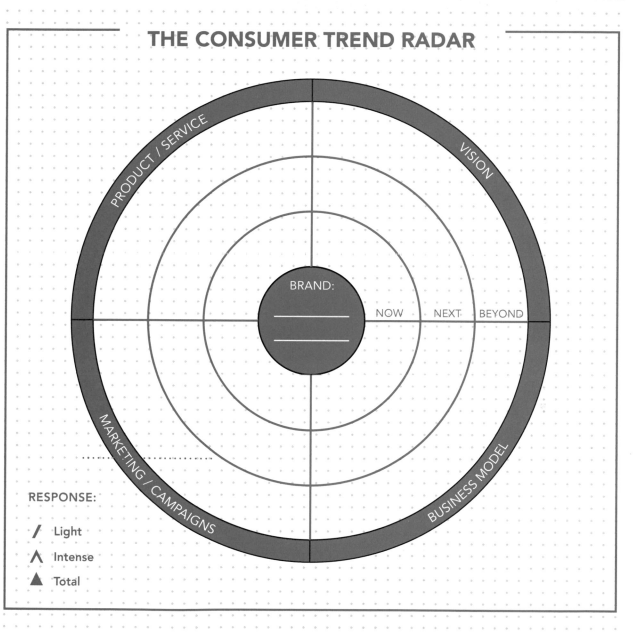

PRODUCT / SERVICE

VISION

BRAND:

_____

_____

NOW   NEXT   BEYOND

MARKETING / CAMPAIGNS

BUSINESS MODEL

RESPONSE:

/ Light

∧ Intense

▲ Total

YOUR CTR SESSIONS

Be guided by your goals, capabilities, and resources.

There's no right answer when it comes to developing your trend-led strategy. That's because your decisions on which trends to apply, when, and how should be based on the specifics of your organization: where it's at now and where you want it to be tomorrow.

TRENDS MEET YOUR BUSINESS

One way to think about the process that is filling in the CTR is that it's where trends meet your long-term goals and short-term aims, your capabilities and resources, and your vision of your own organization. In other words, it's where trends finally meet—and are seen through the lens of—your business.

Filling in the radar can—and should—prompt long (and even heated!) discussion about your organization, what it does, and where it should head next.

Sometimes you'll be able to use your goals and capabilities as fixed points of reference that help you assess a trend: "We have a short-term aim to be more flexible and responsive on pricing, so we should apply this pricing trend now."

But at other times you'll find that thinking around trends is reshaping the very goals, aims, and resource allocation you brought to the table: "I really feel as though this peer-to-peer trend is important, and that's making me think we've neglected the sharing economy in our planning!"

Reevaluation of your organizational planning, then, will form a natural part of your CTR conversations. Embrace that, but remain focused on working toward a single, shared vision of your trend-led strategy.

RED FLAGS

During your CTR discussions, it will pay particular dividends to note when a trend that you feel is important is either:

[i] not reflected in any of your established goals or aims, or

[ii] is a trend that your current capabilities make it very hard or impossible to apply.

When you find such a misalignment, ask: "Why is this important trend not reflected in our goals? Is this a sign we need to change our goals?" or "Why does this important trend not align with our capabilities? What can we do to create the capabilities we need to apply this trend?"

POST-DEMOGRAPHIC COMPLEXITY

And of course, all of these reflections should take place against the backdrop of the Post-Demographic consumer arena described in the previous chapter.

With people freer than ever to construct lifestyles and identities of their choosing, the assumptions and rationales your organization previously used to set priorities need to be replaced by new thinking that accommodates this new Post-Demographic complexity: who your customers are, who they could be, what your brand "ought" to do, and more.

GET STARTED

Before plotting a
trend on the CTR, you
need to ask some key
questions.

To guide your thinking on where
to plot a trend on the CTR, you
need to start by considering how
the trend relates to your goals,
capabilities, resources, and more.
In other words, you need to ask:
"What can this trend do for us?"

Use the questions below to
kickstart discussion. Next, you'll use
the answers you generated to help
you plot the trend on the CTR.

- What are the long-term strategic
  goals for our organization,
  department, or team? How can
  this trend help us achieve or
  revise those goals?

- What are the short-term tactical
  aims for our organization,
  department, or team? How can
  this trend help us achieve or
  revise those aims?

- What are our organization's
  special capabilities? How do they
  impact upon our ability to apply
  this trend, both in terms of timing
  and level of commitment?

- If we lack the competencies and
  capabilities to apply this trend,
  what can we do to change this?

- What resources (including time
  and people) can we dedicate
  to the application of this trend?
  How should this guide how we
  apply the trend?

- If we lack the resources to apply
  this trend, what can we do to
  change this?

- What do our customers—and
  potential customers—expect
  from us? How could this trend
  help us serve those expectations
  or positively change them?

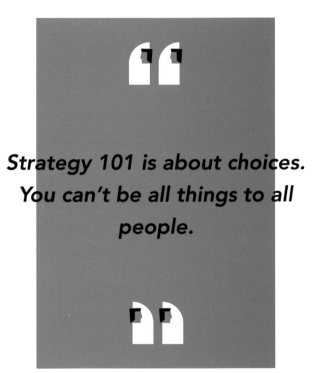

Strategy 101 is about choices. You can't be all things to all people.

Michael Porter

PLOTTING TRENDS

Plot each trend on the
CTR by addressing the
three dimensions.

Once you've discussed how a trend fits into your organization's goals, capabilities, resources, and more—using the questions on the previous page to help—you're ready to plot it on the CTR.

Using the conclusions you generated during your discussion, you must now address the CTR's three dimensions:

[1] **Innovation Target**: in which area of my business will we apply this trend?

[2] **Priority**: when will we apply it?

[3] **Response**: with what level of commitment will we apply it?

The three dimensions are discussed in detail in the next three pages.

IDEATION WITH THE CTR

The CTR is all about planning and prioritizing application of trends. But invariably when you consider a trend against the three dimensions, you'll move toward the beginnings of ideation. Expect thoughts such as: "This trend could help us find our way to new services that reduce waiting time, which is an urgent priority, so I think we should apply this trend soon." Or "I can really see an app now followed by a campaign."

Broad ideation of this kind is a natural part of setting your trend priorities. Just remember, planning and prioritization of trends are the key focus of your sessions with the CTR. There will be plenty of time to move toward specific, concrete innovation ideas when you use the Consumer Trend Canvas, which we'll look at in the next chapter.

[1/3] INNOVATION TARGET

In which area of your business will you apply the trend?

Using the four types of innovation (outlined in SCAN in Chapter 2.2), consider the area(s) of your business that will be the target of this trend. Will you use this trend to reconfigure your entire vision of your business? To generate a new business model? A new product, service, or campaign? Or will it inform new marketing or campaigns?

Of course, many trends can and should impact on more than one— or even all—of these levels. Take the sharing economy as a trend

and BMW's application of that trend in DriveNow, a car-sharing scheme in partnership with car rental company Sixt that makes car-sharing available across a range of European and U.S. cities. DriveNow is a service, but one that also opens the door to a new business model, and one that has allowed BMW to market itself (largely through earned media) as a forward-thinking brand. All set against the emerging vision of BMW as a mobility company rather than an automotive manufacturer.

If you want to apply a trend across more than one Innovation Target, plot the trend on the CTR so that it sits on the border between the two (see how BETTER BUSINESS is plotted in the worked illustration for an example of this).

- Vision
- Business model
- Product/Service
- Marketing/Campaigns

[2/3] PRIORITY

When will you apply the trend?

You can't apply every important trend right away. Which are for now, and which can be left for later?

Of course, there's no single right answer. Timing application of any trend depends on your organization, its goals, aims, and capabilities. For example, just look at how three carmakers have applied the trend for collaborative consumption at different times:

Daimler jumped on the trend for customers to increasingly prefer access over ownership in 2008, when it rolled out its car2go car-sharing scheme, allowing users to rent a Smart car by the hour. Next up was BMW, which waited until 2011 to implement its own play on the trend, with the DriveNow car sharing program (discussed previously). Finally, Audi came to the trend in 2014 via Audi Unite. The pilot program allows Swedish customers to share a car in a private network of up to five people, using an app to keep track of the car's location and availability, and paying either a fixed charge or a fee based on personal usage.

Guided by your goals, aims, and capabilities, choose from three levels of priority: Now, Next, or Beyond.

○ NOW: start today!

◎ NEXT: action within 6 to 24 months. Start planning.

◎ BEYOND: not a priority. Yet.

[3/3] RESPONSE

How intensely will you apply the trend?

In this dimension, you consider your level of commitment to the application of the trend.

How much time do you want to dedicate? How many resources—including money and people—do you want to use? What level of risk are you willing to bear?

Consider those questions against three levels. A light commitment: be experimental; launch new innovations quickly with no excuses. An intense commitment: a considerable investment of time, money, and people. A total commitment: a fundamental shift in your processes or approach.

Take Google's response to the trend for wearable devices. Google Glass was an intense response: one that required time, money, and people, but not a rethink of any fundamentals at the company.

You will notice natural alignments between certain levels and Innovation Targets. For example, when you consider the Innovation Target, if you chose to apply the trend at the level of vision, it is likely that this will require a total commitment. Meanwhile, a product/service application is likely to mean a light or intense response.

/ LIGHT: launch new innovations quickly. No excuses.

∧ INTENSE: requires serious innovation commitment (time, money, people).

△ TOTAL: entails fundamental shifts in mind-set, approach, or vision.

THE CONSUMER TREND RADAR:
HOW TO USE

[EXAMPLE 1/4]

LUXURY AUTOMOTIVE BRAND

This worked example shows where a luxury automotive manufacturer could plot three mega-trends on the CTR.

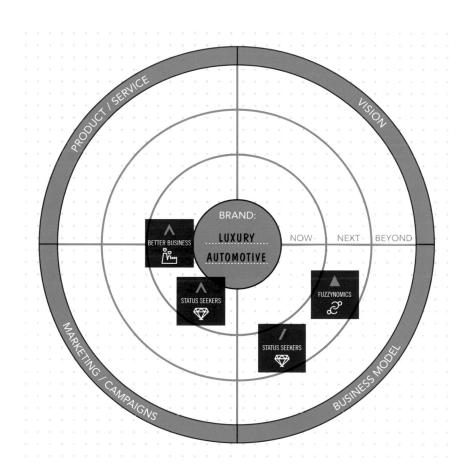

STATUS SEEKERS

The pursuit of status is one of the key drivers of behavior in the consumer arena. But now, consumer status is diversifying toward a range of nonmaterial characteristics: think skills and knowledge, eco-credentials, ethics, taste and sensibility, and more.

MARKETING / NOW / INTENSE

For many, cars are still the ultimate status symbol. Investment in building and supporting the brand's status impact in new ways is a crucial priority for us.

BUSINESS MODEL / NEXT / LIGHT

The diversification of status means cars are losing their position as status signifiers. Adapting to this shift will shape the future of the brand (see FUZZYNOMICS).

BETTER BUSINESS

Rising awareness of the negative impacts of much consumption is driving customers to demand that brands become "better" for society and the environment.

PRODUCT AND MARKETING / NOW / INTENSE

Cars are potent sources of eco-guilt for many customers. We'll need product-line innovations that address this by making our cars less damaging to the planet and other people. But marketing to position us as a responsible luxury choice is also crucial. We need to get going on this now!

FUZZYNOMICS

Driven by the democratization of technologies, tools, and platforms, the boundaries between producers and consumers are rapidly blurring.

BUSINESS MODEL / NEXT / TOTAL

Collaborative consumption models such as car sharing are becoming increasingly attractive to urban customers who prize convenience. The decline in the status attached to car ownership (see STATUS SEEKERS) is likely to only accelerate this shift. We need business model innovation to adapt—but that will take much planning and a big commitment of time and people.

[EXAMPLE 2/4]

FAST FASHION BRAND

This worked example demonstrates where a fast fashion brand could place three trends on the CTR. Each trend is illustrated by an example innovation.

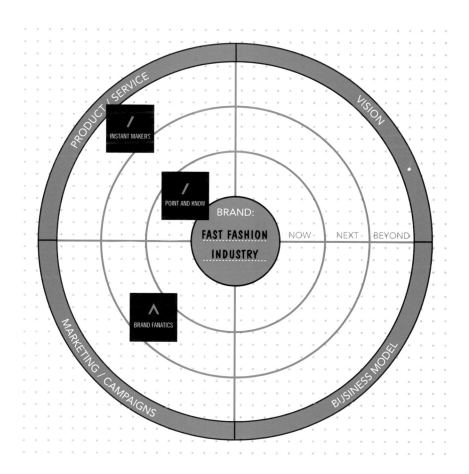

POINT AND KNOW

Smartphone-wielding customers will expect to be able to point their smartphone at any physical object and be instantly informed.

[Example] In April 2014, drinks brand Jose Cuervo launched a free mobile app called History in a Bottle. Users held their smartphone above a bottle of Cuervo Traditional to see an animated 3D history of the brand on their screen.

PRODUCT-SERVICE / NOW / LIGHT
Keeping customers more informed aligns with our long-term move toward transparency. How about experimenting with smartphone-scannable labels, linked to content about our manufacturing or sourcing processes?

INSTANT MAKERS

Fueled by a culture of online creativity, consumers will embrace opportunities to create their own products.

[Example] Launched in the United States in July 2014, Normal allows customers to custom-make their own earphones. Via the Normal app, customers take photographs of both ears using a coin as a point of reference for sizing and select accent colors. The earphones are then 3D-printed for a perfect fit.

PRODUCT-SERVICE / BEYOND / LIGHT
Positioning our brand as one that empowers creativity is another long-term goal. Think in-store custom-printed purses, 3D-printed jewelry, and more. But this requires new capabilities and is lower priority.

BRAND FANATICS

Sophisticated, post-materialist customers are finding ever more outlandish ways to celebrate and champion their favorite brands.

[Example] In August 2014, IKEA ran a competition inviting its Malaysian fans to dress up as their favorite IKEA products. A total of 127 people took part in the contest to win store vouchers, with participants dressing up as items such as the Fnitter wall clock and Haggas pendant lamp, and submitting their pictures via Facebook.

MARKETING-CAMPAIGNS / NEXT / INTENSE
We already have a well-developed community of brand fans. What about a series of fan events across key cities, which form the basis of an online campaign? Let's engage our creative agency.

HOW TO USE

[EXAMPLE 3/4]
FMCG
RETAILER

This worked example demonstrates where a Fast-Moving Consumer Goods retailer could place three trends on the CTR. Each trend is illustrated by an example innovation.

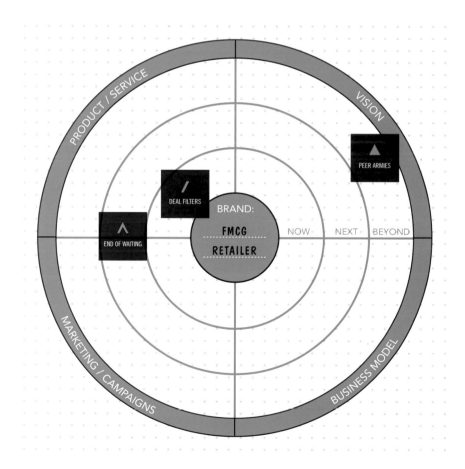

END OF WAITING

Fueled by the instant nature of the digital space, customer tolerance for waiting is falling to zero. Brands should identify customer wait times, and then kill it or fill it.

[Example] In October 2014, Starbucks piloted an "order ahead" function in its app across 150 stores in Portland. Users could order a coffee at a designated store and time, allowing them to skip the in-store queue.

PRODUCT/SERVICE AND MARKETING CAMPAIGN / NEXT / INTENSE
Making lives more convenient is a key way to differentiate our brand. Let's brainstorm around in-store and online/order ahead service. How can we champion these innovations via a campaign built around zero waiting?

PEER ARMIES

Businesses are leveraging networks of ordinary people (i.e. non-employees) to supercharge their customer service.

[Example] During the FIFA World Cup in June 2014, Brazilian beer brand Skol launched Consulado, a platform connecting locals with visiting tourists. Locals who helped visitors navigate their city were rewarded with discounts on bottles of Skol.

VISION / BEYOND / TOTAL
The trend aligns perfectly with our long-term goal to become a brand that offers customers a personal touch, including help with delivery from brand representatives. Could networks of peers allow us to do this in a new, more effective way? Needs serious thought.

DEAL FILTERS

Deal overload has become a new form of information overload. Consumers are searching for services that help them filter only the deals they want.

[Example] Launched in August 2014, fashion app Grabble allows users to browse fashion collections and swipe right on an item to receive an alert when it is discounted.

PRODUCT-SERVICE / NOW / LIGHT
Customers tell us our deals are hard to navigate. We have the technical capacity to quickly roll out a digital service to help customers filter deals based on their personal preferences.

[EXAMPLE 4/4]
TRENDWATCHING

This worked example
shows how we at
TrendWatching
recently plotted three
mega-trends that
are important to our
future on the CTR.

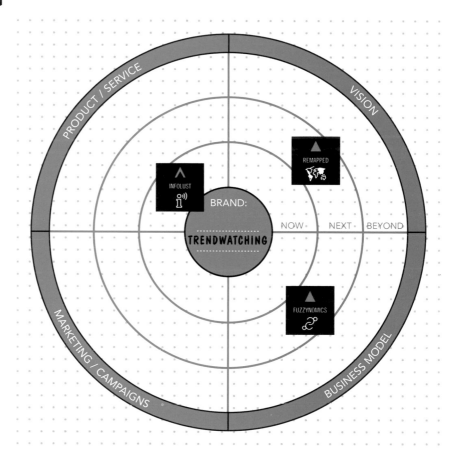

FUZZYNOMICS

Driven by the democratization of technologies, tools, and platforms, the boundaries between producers and consumers are rapidly blurring.

BUSINESS MODEL / NEXT / TOTAL
We already crowdsource many innovations from TW:IN, our global network of trend spotters. How could we transform the network to exponentially increase the number and quality of submissions, allowing us to provide entirely new kinds of crowd-powered insight?

INFOLUST

Consumers will continue to embrace tools that offer them entertaining and useful information in new and compelling ways.

PRODUCT-SERVICE / NOW / INSTENSE
Of course, trend information is what we've always been about! But this mega-trend aligns with our aim to share powerful data on how our readers interact with trends. Think heat maps of important trends by industry and region, user-generated insight, and more.

REMAPPED

The rise of a multipolar global economy is not just expanding consumer markets, it's creating new processes, structures, business models, and brands.

VISION / NEXT / TOTAL
A fundamental part of our vision for the months and years ahead is that we increase our international presence and our ability to deliver global insight with local relevance—a demanding and ongoing commitment.

BUILDING YOUR TREND-LED STRATEGY

We don't claim that it's easy to complete the CTR. Talking through your important trends and agreeing where to plot them against the three dimensions means addressing—and finding agreement on—fundamental questions about your organization's capabilities, mission, and future. It takes time and effort. But dedicate that time and effort and you'll be more than paid back: by the process itself, and the end result that is your completed CTR.

First, the process will encourage— or rather, force—you and your team to confront hidden assumptions that have guided your decision making in the past. You'll then have to commit to a shared vision of how the business should move forward.

It should also be exciting. The structured process will help your organization uncover dimensions and new opportunities that you hadn't previously considered. And seeing the results visually will help get people on board.

And second, once you have been through the process and have a completed radar, you'll have an embodiment of the plan you have settled on. A simplification of a more complex reality, yes; but one that will set a clear path to direct and encourage concrete action in the months and years ahead.

Share it with colleagues, stick it on walls, put it on the company intranet. And then get going!

> **NEXT**

Having read this chapter, you now:

[1] Understand the Consumer Trend Radar (CTR) and its three dimensions; and

[2] Can run a successful CTR session and create a visual, shareable map of your trend-led strategy for the months and years ahead.

....

That draws the FOCUS section to a close. Equipped to choose the trends you'll run with and plan their application, you're now ready for GENERATE, where you'll learn how to turn trends into innovations that consumers will love.

....

GENERATE

TURN INSIGHTS INTO IDEAS

[GENERATE]

Spotting the latest trends and correctly identifying which are relevant to your business is a complete waste of time if you then don't use those insights to launch innovations that keep you ahead of customers' accelerating expectations.

That's why we created the Consumer Trend Canvas (CTC), a simple yet powerful tool that walks you through the process of trend-driven ideation from analysis to application.

After reading this section, you'll be able to turn your trend insights into compelling new business, product, service, and marketing opportunities, both on your own and also—because innovation is a team effort—by running successful ideation sessions with your team or clients.

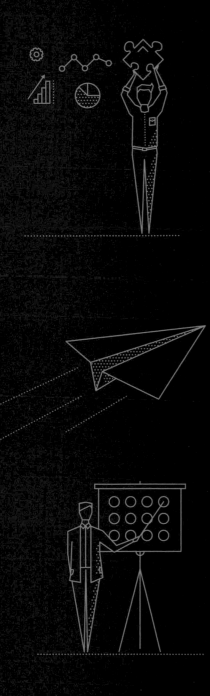

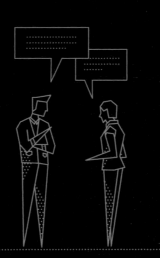

THE CONSUMER TREND CANVAS

A simple tool for generating compelling, trend-driven innovation ideas.

The Consumer Trend Canvas (CTC) is an easy-to-follow, one-page tool that walks you through a trend and helps you move from insight to innovation.

At its core are all the elements we've covered so far in this book. We've honed both the canvas and the underlying methodology that supports it during the 10-plus years that we've been trying to make trends and their application more accessible. This methodology has been battle-tested during our work with hundreds of leading brands, agencies, consultancies, schools, nonprofits, and more across six continents. It works.

It works because it's simple. It divides the process of working with a trend into two main parts: analysis and application. It guides you to ask the right questions. It pushes you to examine examples of your chosen trend in action. It lays out the three core elements of a trend—basic needs, drivers of change, and innovations—in order to help you assess how these components fit together and create new expectations. It prompts you to think about where, how, and for whom you will apply the trend to create new customers and delight existing ones.

The canvas will help you not only understand a trend better, but also ensure that your new initiatives are deeply grounded in what customers want, desire, and expect.

Let's see how.

HOW TO USE

The two-minute
overview.

[1] **Download a blank canvas.**
Print off the CTC template, the
bigger the better. If you're running
a group session check out
Chapter 4.3 for detailed tips on how
to run successful ideation workshops.

[2] **Choose a trend.**
If you've followed the Trend-Driven
Innovation process up to this point,
you will already have a shortlist
of trends that you're focusing on.
Alternatively, you may just be
interested in exploring a trend you
read about online or saw presented
at a conference. Either works.

[3] **Start with ANALYZE.**
This is where you unpack the trend.
Look at real-world examples of the
trend (Inspiration). Then turn to the
Drivers of Change that brought it
about, the Basic Needs it taps into,
and the Emerging Expectations
it reflects. Use Post-its to capture
your insights so you can move and
edit them easily.

[4] **Turn to APPLY.**
Now it's time to consider the trend
in the context of your business.
Identify how, where, and for whom
you will apply the trend. Refer

back to the insights you generated
during the analysis phase. Make
connections between the two
halves of the canvas to uncover
truly novel concepts.

[5] **Capture your innovation idea.**
Congratulations! Your new idea
will be deeply aligned with what
tomorrow's customers will want,
and is destined to delight.

....

**Let's walk through each step in
more detail, using the GUILT-FREE
CONSUMPTION trend.**

....

Head online to download a blank template.

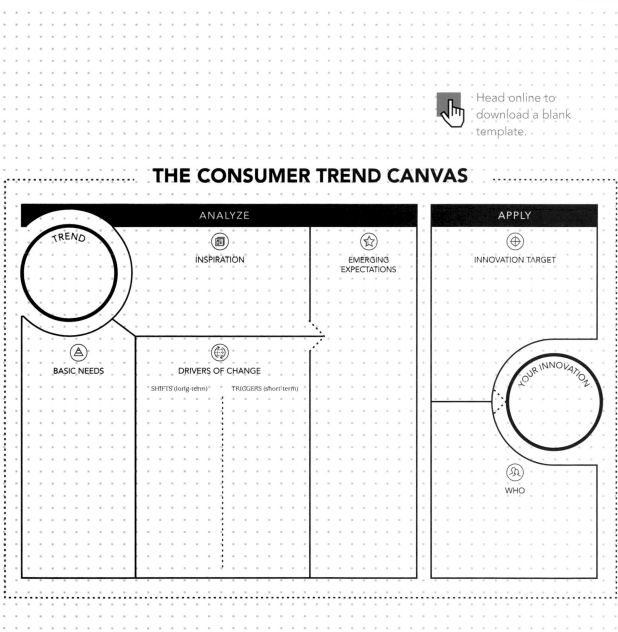

THE CONSUMER TREND CANVAS

ANALYZE

TREND

INSPIRATION

EMERGING EXPECTATIONS

BASIC NEEDS

DRIVERS OF CHANGE

SHIFTS (long-term)   TRIGGERS (short-term)

APPLY

INNOVATION TARGET

YOUR INNOVATION

WHO

WORKED EXAMPLE

GUILT-FREE CONSUMPTION

Thanks to ever-greater awareness as to the impact of their actions, people are increasingly wracked with guilt about their consumption habits. The result? A growing hunger for a new kind of consumerism: one free from worry about its negative impact, while still allowing continued indulgence.

We touched on the GUILT-FREE CONSUMPTION trend in the book's introduction.

At the heart of this trend is the notion that people want to be good. They want to feel good about themselves and the impact they have on the world—or at least not feel *bad* about it. Yet it's now almost impossible for any individual to claim ignorance over the havoc his or her consumption is and has been wreaking.

However, a very human mix of desire, indulgence, addiction, and genuine pleasure (fueled by everything from tasty Whoppers to low-cost city breaks to shiny phablets) stops people from substantially changing their behavior. At the same time, a host of new brands shows that ethical and responsible practices *can* be compatible with business success.

These forces fuel the tension that manifests itself in the potent, nagging guilt trip haunting many consumers today. But the same tension offers huge opportunities to those who can resolve it.

THE CONSUMER TREND CANVAS

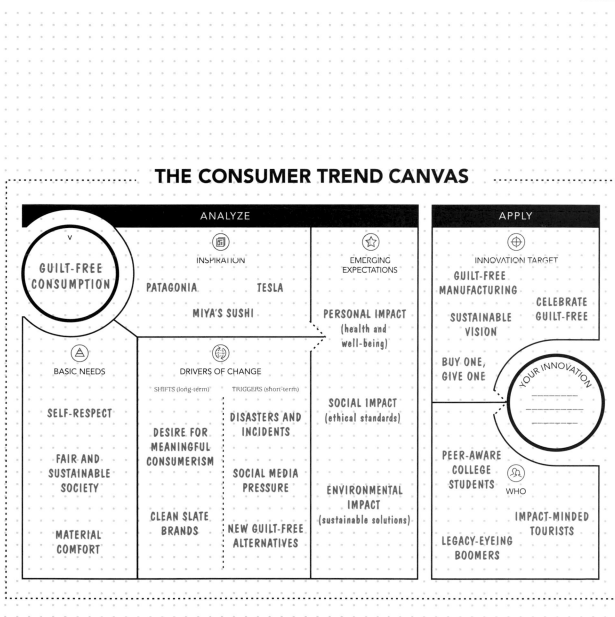

ANALYZE

GUILT-FREE CONSUMPTION

INSPIRATION

PATAGONIA   TESLA

MIYA'S SUSHI

EMERGING EXPECTATIONS

PERSONAL IMPACT (health and well-being)

BASIC NEEDS

SELF-RESPECT

FAIR AND SUSTAINABLE SOCIETY

MATERIAL COMFORT

DRIVERS OF CHANGE

SHIFTS (long-term)   TRIGGERS (short-term)

DESIRE FOR MEANINGFUL CONSUMERISM

CLEAN SLATE BRANDS

DISASTERS AND INCIDENTS

SOCIAL MEDIA PRESSURE

NEW GUILT-FREE ALTERNATIVES

SOCIAL IMPACT (ethical standards)

ENVIRONMENTAL IMPACT (sustainable solutions)

APPLY

INNOVATION TARGET

GUILT-FREE MANUFACTURING

SUSTAINABLE VISION

CELEBRATE GUILT-FREE

BUY ONE, GIVE ONE

YOUR INNOVATION

_____
_____
_____

PEER-AWARE COLLEGE STUDENTS

WHO

IMPACT-MINDED TOURISTS

LEGACY-EYEING BOOMERS

[ANALYZE]

INSPIRATION

How are other businesses
applying this trend?

We've demonstrated how looking at how other actors (from new startups to large corporations) are *already* applying a trend is a great way to gauge how current offerings will raise customer expectations. Here's a quick recap of some guilt-free initiatives featured previously:

PATAGONIA

The outdoor clothing company has consistently pushed a guilt-free environmental agenda: the company's Footprint Chronicles blog freely publishes details of its supply chain, while its 2011 "Don't Buy This Jacket" Black Friday campaign was a legendary jab at wasteful consumerism.

MIYA'S SUSHI

Sushi lovers often struggle with guilt, given the notoriously fragile position of many fish stocks. Miya's Sushi goes beyond not including endangered fish on its menu: it offers dishes made with nonnative, invasive species that are damaging the local habitat. Therefore, eating them is positively *protecting* local species. How's that for GUILT-FREE?

TESLA

The Model S perfectly epitomizes the GUILT-FREE trend: the all-electric sports car going some way to bridging the seemingly irreconcilable tension between high-speed, high-status automotive indulgence and concern for the environment. It became the first electric car to top the monthly new car sales ranking in any country, leading the table multiple times in Norway (while breaking national records).

INSPIRATION

PATAGONIA

MIYA'S SUSHI

TESLA

[ANALYZE]

BASIC NEEDS

Which deep consumer needs and desires does this trend address?

Consumer trends are always rooted in basic, fundamental human needs and desires. Identifying these is central to understanding any trend. So, what are the basic needs when it comes to GUILT-FREE CONSUMPTION?

One is to feel good about oneself, and people feel good about themselves when they live according to deeply held values. These include aspirations for a fair and ethical society, and for environmentally sustainable lifestyles.

Indeed, while these values might not always be reflected in people's choices and behavior on a daily basis, we are fundamentally optimistic about human nature and confident that, all other things being equal, these *are* universal values.

Of course, people also want to have a materially comfortable life. This is why movements that call for a total rejection of consumerism are doomed to failure: we like our sushi and our sports cars too much!

[TIP] Struggling to come up with the basic needs and wants for a trend? Turn to Chapter 2.1 for a summary of the major ones.

BASIC NEEDS

SELF-RESPECT

FAIR AND
SUSTAINABLE
SOCIETY

MATERIAL
COMFORT

[ANALYZE]

DRIVERS OF CHANGE

Why is this trend emerging now?
What's changing?

Trends always involve change, too. As discussed in Chapter 2.1, change can be analyzed in terms of "Shifts" (long-term, macro changes playing out across years or even decades) and "Triggers" (more immediate or specific changes). What are the Shifts and Triggers driving the GUILT-FREE trend?

SHIFTS:

The world continues to become ever more transparent. Customers are now better informed about all kinds of impacts, from the effect of logging on the environment, to the role of refined sugar in the obesity epidemic, to working conditions on the far side of the world.

Mass affluence and overwhelming material abundance has led people to seek personal expression, meaning, and self-actualization in their consumption.

The success of Patagonia, Tesla, and other CLEAN SLATE BRANDS (built on foundations of ethical and responsible business practices) has only highlighted the deeply flawed nature of many conventional products and brands.

TRIGGERS:

People's guilt triggers are often personal but also include: hearing about tragic incidents (from garment factory collapses to oil tanker beachings), media exposés of guilt-laden supply chains, and new guilt-free alternative products, all set against a backdrop of instant and vocal social media outrage.

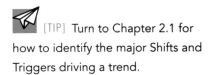 [TIP] Turn to Chapter 2.1 for how to identify the major Shifts and Triggers driving a trend.

DRIVERS OF CHANGE

SHIFTS (long-term)	TRIGGERS (short-term)
	DISASTERS AND INCIDENTS
DESIRE FOR MEANINGFUL CONSUMERISM	
	SOCIAL MEDIA PRESSURE
CLEAN SLATE BRANDS	
	NEW GUILT-FREE ALTERNATIVES

[ANALYZE]

EMERGING EXPECTATIONS

What points of tension and new
customer expectations are emerging?

You know by now that trends emerge when basic human needs, external change, and new offerings combine to create new expectations among customers.

Understanding a trend and the opportunities it presents is all about finding points of tension between what people currently have and what they want or expect.

Underpinning the GUILT-FREE CONSUMPTION trend is the growing tension between the kind of consumption that customers would like (one that allows them to continue to enjoy themselves without—or with less—worry about the impact of that consumption) and the kind of consumption they too often find themselves left with.

Now, most people don't expect *no* impact, but they *do* expect businesses to have taken steps to minimize (if not eliminate) as much of the negative impact as possible. Businesses are now *expected* to minimize environmental damage and generate sustainable solutions. Businesses are *expected* to give back, and use their resources to generate value for society, not just their shareholders. And, rather than exploit people's worst vices, businesses are *expected* to consider how to help customers to help themselves become healthier, smarter, and happier.

[TIP] Chapter 2.2 (Watch Businesses First, Customers Second) explains in detail how to identify emerging customer expectations using new business innovations.

EMERGING
EXPECTATIONS

PERSONAL IMPACT
(health and well-being)

SOCIAL IMPACT
(ethical standards)

ENVIRONMENTAL
IMPACT
(sustainable solutions)

[APPLY]

INNOVATION TARGET

How and where could you apply this trend to your business?

Just as you can use the four types of innovation to analyze new initiatives and spot trends, you can use the same framework to think about where you will apply a trend:

[a] **Long-term Vision:** is your company's long-term vision oriented around minimizing negative impacts, or even contributing positively and being part of the solution?

[b] **Business Model:** could you adopt a more guilt-free business model? Look at Collaborative Economy models, which aim to reduce the need for new materials by using existing assets and resources as efficiently as possible. Or a "buy one, give one" model, as pioneered by TOMS shoes?

[c] **Product / Service:** can you remove as much of the personal, social, and environmental guilt as possible from your manufacturing, distribution, and consumption processes?

[d] **Marketing:** how can you publicly celebrate the guilt-free initiatives that you have (hopefully!) pursued?

 [TIP] Reference example innovations to see how the trend is being applied across the four types (this is why it helps to spot a diverse range of innovations).

INNOVATION TARGET

SUSTAINABLE
VISION

GUILT-FREE
MANUFACTURING

CELEBRATE
GUILT-FREE

BUY ONE,
GIVE ONE

[APPLY]

WHO

Which (new) customer groups could you apply this trend to?

The businesses that create new levels of expectation often serve very specific customer segments, at least initially. Patagonia targeted climbers. Tesla targeted wealthy Californian entrepreneurs. When applying a trend, think about what changes you would have to make to make it relevant for other (new) customer segments.

Once you have chosen your target customer segments, revisit the other sections of the canvas. Knowing whom you want to reach will help you uncover more specific

points of tension. A new father will look for pesticide-free baby food, while a high-flying executive is more concerned about her carbon footprint as a result of frequent business travel commitments.

Which other customer segments would embrace GUILT-FREE CONSUMPTION? Think how you could cater to impact-minded tourists, legacy-eyeing boomers, peer-aware college students, or others afflicted by potent guilt. Absolve them!

[TIP] Check out the **Customer Profile** from *Value Proposition Design*. It builds upon Clayton Christensen's "jobs-to-be-done" framework and encourages you to assess the "pains" and "gains" of your target customer.

PEER-AWARE
COLLEGE
STUDENTS

WHO

IMPACT-MINDED
TOURISTS

LEGACY-EYEING
BOOMERS

[APPLY]

YOUR INNOVATION

Congratulations! You've just experienced Trend-Driven Innovation!

By this point you (and your team) *will* have come up with all kinds of innovation ideas. Because these were driven by the insights you generated when unpacking the trend, they'll be deeply anchored in basic human needs while still being firmly focused on resolving points of tension arising out of changes in the consumer and business arenas. As a result they'll be relevant to customers, and have a greater chance of success.

Which, in the end, is the reason for watching trends in the first place!

 Head online to download an Innovation Worksheet.

YOUR INNOVATION

INNOVATION NAME

BRAND

DESCRIPTION

INNOVATION TYPE:

Product / Service .... ○

New Business Model .... ○

Vision .... ○

Marketing .... ○

CONSUMER EXPECTATION GAP

WHO IS IT FOR

> **NEXT**

Having read this chapter, you now:

[1] Know how to use the Consumer Trend Canvas,
a simple one-page tool that walks you through
generating compelling ideas from trend insights; and

[2] Have seen how the Consumer Trend Canvas can be
used to unpack a trend, GUILT-FREE CONSUMPTION
in this case.

....

Next, let's look at how using the Consumer Trend Canvas
will help you generate compelling new business model,
product, service, and campaign ideas.

....

THE CONSUMER TREND CANVAS IN ACTION

Practical examples to learn from.

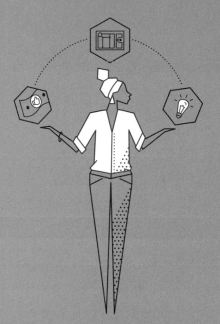

Now that you've seen the theory of the Consumer Trend Canvas, let's take it one step further and demonstrate exactly how the CTC will help you generate compelling new innovation ideas.

Over the following pages, we will introduce you to three more trends—SYMPATHETIC PRICING, M2P (Mentor-to-Protégé), and BRANDED GOVERNMENT—and a selection of recent innovations that illustrate them.

We'll use the CTC to unpack each trend into its constituent parts before imagining how two brands could turn these insights into novel, trend-driven innovation ideas.

Then once your mind is fired up with possibilities, we'll hear how one entrepreneur used the canvas and our CURRENCIES OF CHANGE trend to direct and validate her research when conceiving her new venture.

Your job as you read this chapter? To constantly think about where, how, and for whom *you* might apply these trends yourself. But enough talk, let's see it in action!

TRENDS UNPACKED

[TREND 1/3]

SYMPATHETIC PRICING

Flexible and imaginative discounts that help ease lifestyle pain points, lend a helping hand in difficult times, or support a shared value.

An endless stream of brands claim to care about people and their everyday challenges, or the shared problems of sustainability and social responsibility. Yet many customers see this growing message saturation as all talk. In Europe, only 5 percent of brands are seen to make a meaningful difference in people's lives. In America, it is 9 percent.

Yet amid this deep skepticism, people still have a basic desire for HUMAN BRANDS that show some empathy and compassion.

Meanwhile, as pricing has become ever more fluid, it has triggered customers (who've *always* sought bargains) to expect dynamic, intelligent, real-time pricing, certainly online, but increasingly offline, too.

The SYMPATHETIC PRICING trend sits at the convergence of these forces, capturing the opportunities for organizations that are prepared to put their money where their mouth is and offer discounts and deals that *prove* they care.

INSPIRATION

Check out the businesses
that are already applying
the trend.

SOUTH CHINA MORNING POST

PAYWALL DROPPED DURING PROTEST

In September 2014, the *South
China Morning Post* newspaper
took down its paywall to give
readers free coverage of Occupy
Central, Hong Kong's pro-
democracy movement. As a result,
the site crashed after receiving such
a high volume of traffic.

UBER

DISCOUNTS DURING DISRUPTION

In 2013, the company offered free
rides to students in Boston during a
24-hour bus strike. Similarly, during
a 48-hour subway strike in London,
people who split their fare with
other passengers would receive a
50 percent discount on their trip.

BGH

HOT DEALS ON AIR CONDITIONERS

In late 2013, Argentinian brand
BGH launched its Mi Casa Es Un
Horno ("My Home Is an Oven")
campaign. A dedicated site allowed
people to calculate how exposed
to the sun their apartment was. The
longer the exposure, the higher the
discount they could claim.

[A]
ANALYZE

The left-hand side of the canvas helps us to understand the core components of the trend.

ANALYZE

TREND

SYMPATHETIC PRICING

INSPIRATION

UBER

SOUTH CHINA MORNING POST   BGH

EMERGING EXPECTATIONS

BASIC NEEDS

DRIVERS OF CHANGE

SHIFTS (long-term)   TRIGGERS (short-term)

PERSONALIZATION

VALUE FOR MONEY

CONNECTION

LIVE BY ONE'S VALUES

PURPOSEFUL CONSUMERISM

MESSAGE SATURATION

SKEPTICISM

E-COMMERCE AND M-COMMERCE:

- FLEXIBLE PRICING
- DATA-LED TARGETING

REAL-TIME RESPONSIVENESS

COMPASSIONATE BRANDS

[B]
APPLY

Here is how two different businesses might apply this trend:

1. Sports broadcaster
Encourage sports fans to register their favorite team on the pay-per-view app. When the team loses a game, the fan receives a Commiseration Coupon to watch their next game for half-price.

2. Low-cost airline
During winter months, the airline offers Rain Runaways, with flights to warmer destinations available at discounts; the size of the discount being determined by how much it has rained that day.

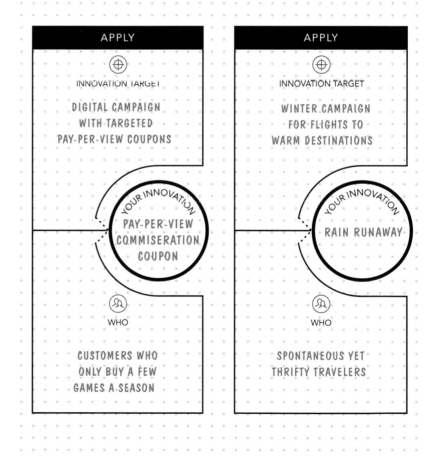

[TREND 2/3]

M2P

(Mentor-to-Protégé) Customers will embrace ways to quickly and easily connect with personal mentors who have the knowledge, skills, and experience they seek.

As discussed in prior chapters, humans have an innate desire to better themselves, whether it's their productivity, fitness, or mindfulness. And self-improvement should now be easier than ever.

First, the proliferation of tracking technology (in running shoes, wristbands, and especially in smartphones) is providing people with detailed and ubiquitous personal data that can be used to set goals and monitor progress.

Second, there is now a host of platforms that have democratized

learning. However, limited personal accountability or encouragement can make motivation an issue. Indeed, lack of mentor contact is cited as a prime reason for the dismal completion rates by students of massive open online courses (MOOCs).

At the same time, people expect brands to empower them, and they expect instant digital connection (as evidenced by brands from Tinder to Snapchat). Smart brands will meet these two expectations while facilitating self-improvement.

INSPIRATION

Check out the businesses that are already applying the trend.

GOQii

FITNESS TRACKER LINKS TO TRAINER

Launched in India in 2014, the GOQii fitness tracker connects users directly to a real personal trainer to push them to reach their goals. Data from the wristband is shared with a trainer who uses the information to offer personalized tips and encouragement.

CODEMENTOR

INSTANT VIDEO HELP FOR CODERS

Codementor, launched in 2014, connects those struggling with a programming problem with expert developers. Users post a problem in the online marketplace and then connect to specialists to work together via screen-sharing, video, and text chat.

RISE

TOUGH LOVE FROM NUTRITIONISTS

Rise is a dietary advisory service. Users connect with a nutritionist via the mobile app and receive a customized weight loss plan. Users share a photo diary of their meals and receive feedback from their coach, with options ranging from "supportive" to "tough love."

[A]
ANALYZE

ANALYZE

TREND
M2P

INSPIRATION

RISE   CODEMENTOR

GOQii

EMERGING EXPECTATIONS

BASIC NEEDS

SELF-IMPROVEMENT

CONNECTION

VALIDATION

DRIVERS OF CHANGE

SHIFTS (long-term)   TRIGGERS (short-term)

FOCUS ON HEALTHY LIVING

KNOWLEDGE- AND SKILL-BASED ECONOMIES

ADVANCES IN WEARABLES

SELF-TRACKING TECH

ADOPTION OF MOBILE SOCIAL PLATFORMS

INSTANT SOCIAL CONNECTION

BRANDS <u>MUST</u> EMPOWER CONSUMERS

[B]
APPLY

1. Kitchenware manufacturer
Pots and pans are sold with a voucher entitling the buyer to a personal video tutorial (via tablet or mobile app) with a professional chef using the specific product. Personalized "virtual cooking school" packages are available as a product extension.

2. Mobile gaming developer
Create a feature where gamers can purchase credits to receive live voice-chat tips during gameplay from highly ranked players (masters). Users rank the quality of the tips, and the masters receive in-game currency in return.

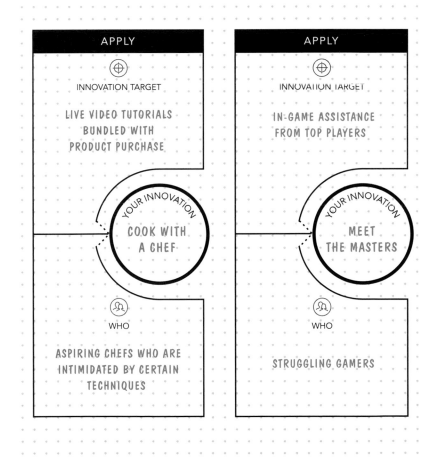

[TREND 3/3]

BRANDED GOVERNMENT

People around the world will increasingly look to progressive brands to step up and become effective agents of local civic transformation: brands that work with, or make up for a lack of, public services.

Citizens have a basic need and even a dependency on public infrastructure that enables them to lead safe and comfortable lives.

Yet many local and national governments in the developed world are facing financial shortfalls, while emerging market authorities struggle to keep up with the explosive demand for public services and infrastructure.

Exacerbating this is the increasing transparency on the activities and output of governments around the world. Citizens who see or hear about better services abroad quickly become frustrated with their domestic equivalent.

Meanwhile on a global basis, citizens now trust businesses more than governments, and a majority expect businesses to contribute to—and bear responsibility for— driving positive social change as much as governments.

As a result, businesses that deliver valuable and trustworthy public services will be increasingly welcome.

INSPIRATION

Check out the businesses
that are already applying
the trend.

DIAL DIRECT
FILLING IN THE GAPS

South African insurer Dial Direct
launched the Pothole Brigade,
a popular road maintenance
initiative. It repaired over
50,000 potholes in and around
Johannesburg between 2011 and
2012, before bureaucratic issues
caused the initiative to be halted.

CIF
RACIST GRAFFITI REMOVAL

In 2014, cleaning product Cif
asked Romanians to submit photos
of racist graffiti via an app. The
brand then sent a cleaning team to
remove the graffiti, posting before
and after photos to an online map.
In the four-month campaign, 385
locations were cleaned.

TORTRIX
"EMBASSY" FOR JOBSEEKERS

Residents of Zona 18 in Guatemala
are often stigmatized because
gangs control the area. Snack
brand Tortrix and nonprofit Area 18
created an "embassy" for residents,
giving them an alternative address
to use on résumés when job
seeking to avoid discrimination.

[A]
ANALYZE

ANALYZE		
TREND **BRANDED GOVERNMENT**	**INSPIRATION** CLEAN ROMANIA / CIF EMBAJADA ZONA 18 / TORTRIX POTHOLE BRIGADE / DIAL DIRECT	**EMERGING EXPECTATIONS**
BASIC NEEDS TRUST AND CONFIDENCE BELONGING SAFETY AND PROTECTION	**DRIVERS OF CHANGE** SHIFTS (long-term) / TRIGGERS (short-term) TRANSPARENCY / CIVIC PROTESTS (REAL AND ON SOCIAL MEDIA) MULTINATIONALS CAPABLE OF LARGE-SCALE IMPACT / AUSTERITY	TRUST GAP POSITIVE CONTRIBUTION AND INVESTMENT IN SOCIETY

[B]
APPLY

1. Multinational diaper brand

Many parents in urban areas struggle to afford day care that would allow them to work full time. To counter this, the brand will subsidize the creation of new facilities in a selected city, with a goal of doubling access to affordable day care within five years.

2. Athletic brand

Pledge to repair and refurbish four inner-city basketball courts a month. Local players submit their own court for consideration with a tagged Vine or Instagram video that shows why their court deserves to be repaired.

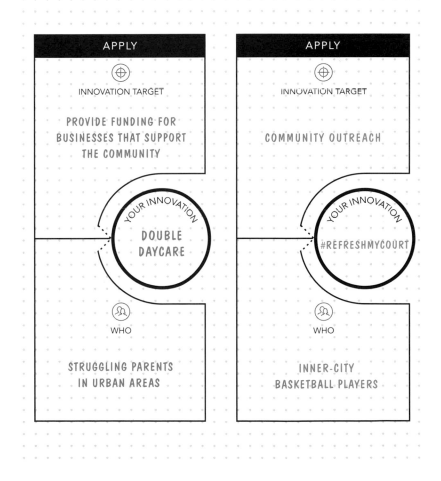

APPLY

INNOVATION TARGET

PROVIDE FUNDING FOR BUSINESSES THAT SUPPORT THE COMMUNITY

YOUR INNOVATION

DOUBLE DAYCARE

WHO

STRUGGLING PARENTS IN URBAN AREAS

APPLY

INNOVATION TARGET

COMMUNITY OUTREACH

YOUR INNOVATION

#REFRESHMYCOURT

WHO

INNER-CITY BASKETBALL PLAYERS

PERSONAL HEROES

How a startup can take
a trend and the CTC to
sharpen their focus.

PersonalHeroes is an Israeli startup
that has developed an index for
kindness.

The service is based around a
mobile app that allows users to tag
and reward people doing "good"
actions, such as giving someone
back their wallet.

Corporate partners who wish to
support kindness (the pilot program
was with Coca-Cola) can then offer
rewards—from virtual badges to
real-world discounts—to individuals
who have performed good deeds.

[TREND]

CURRENCIES OF CHANGE

Customers on a never-ending quest for self-improvement will embrace ever more personal, innovative, fun, timely, targeted, and ultimately relevant rewards and discounts that incentivize a desired behavior.

We know in materially affluent societies, where basic needs are easily met, human motivation quickly shifts away from "what I have" to "who I am." The result is the relentless pursuit of personal self-improvement across countless axes: health, skills and knowledge, creativity, ethics, values, and many more.

The problem? Other, self-sabotaging impulses and faults that are just as much a part of human nature: lack of motivation, low visibility, loss of focus, and yes,

plain old laziness (hey, we're all guilty at times).

Digital self-tracking promised to revolutionize behavior, but data alone wasn't enough. Instead, forward-thinking actors will combine the data generated by the widespread and habitual use of ultrapersonal devices with a deep understanding of human nature to offer more relevant and therefore more compelling rewards, and in the process help people change themselves for the better.

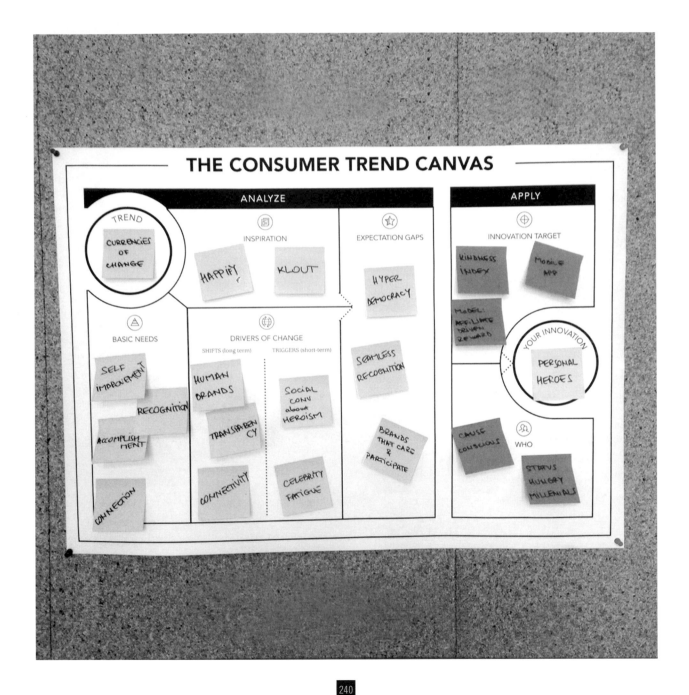

THE CONSUMER TREND CANVAS

ANALYZE

APPLY

TREND

CURRENCIES
OF
CHANGE

INSPIRATION

HAPPIFY

KLOUT

EXPECTATION GAPS

HYPER
DEMOCRACY

INNOVATION TARGET

KINDNESS
INDEX

MOBILE
APP

MODEL:
AFFILIATE
DRIVEN
REWARD

BASIC NEEDS

SELF
IMPROVEMENT

RECOGNITION

ACCOMPLISH
MENT

CONNECTION

DRIVERS OF CHANGE

SHIFTS (long term)

TRIGGERS (short-term)

HUMAN
BRANDS

TRANSPAREN
CY

CONNECTIVITY

SOCIAL
CONV
about
HEROISM

CELEBRITY
FATIGUE

SEAMLESS
RECOGNITION

BRANDS
THAT CARE
&
PARTICIPATE

YOUR INNOVATION

PERSONAL
HEROES

CAUSE
CONSCIOUS

WHO

STATUS
HUNGRY
MILLENIALS

STEPHIE KNOPEL, FOUNDER

Stephie Knopel, founder of PersonalHeroes, explained how she used the Consumer Trend Canvas to develop the concept:

"I remember having a strong intuition about the main vision for PersonalHeroes and how the conversation around 'kindness' was developing in different directions and was a powerful cross-cultural trend. But it wasn't until we deeply analyzed the Drivers of Change with the canvas that we understood the fascinating nature of this space. We looked at data around changing attitudes (just one statistic among many: 42 percent of millennials expect to "use social media to change the world for the better" more in the future than they do today), high volumes of social engagement around everyday heroism (just search Instagram and Pinterest for #GoodDeed), and more. And importantly, how empty it was of other players. Technology enables us to measure and track almost everything in life: social influence (Klout), happiness (Happify), and even our breathing (Spire). But there was little about kindness, about how good you are and how that could influence your reputation.

"Doing a cross check with the emerging expectations confirmed for us the shift toward the idea that anyone can be a hero, and can—and should—be rewarded for their actions.

"This all combined to trigger our 'aha' moment! We are bringing science, data, and transparency to kindness. The product might iterate thousands of times, but the vision won't change."

❯ **NEXT**

Having read this chapter, you now:

[1] Have seen how a range of businesses can use the Consumer Trend Canvas to generate ideas across a variety of trends; and

[2] Should have a number of ideas for new business concepts, products, services, and campaigns of your own!

....

Next, let's look at how to get your colleagues involved, by running successful ideation sessions using the Consumer Trend Canvas.

....

TREND-DRIVEN IDEATION SESSIONS

Run workshops that deliver winning ideas.

While you can work with trends by yourself, it's likely that at some point you will want and need to bring others on board.

Having people use a trend to come up with new ideas for your organization is a great way to turn them on to the power of trend-driven innovation. People enjoy flexing their creative muscles. And once they have undergone the process of using trends to uncover potential opportunities (and seen how simple it can be), then they'll be hungry to continue!

We've run countless trend and innovation sessions over the years, with organizations as diverse as 3M, Accenture, the BBC, Estée Lauder, Intel, Universal Music, and WWF. In this chapter we'll share exactly how we approach these and how we use the Consumer Trend Canvas to trigger meaningful customer-centered innovation ideas.

Follow along, and we guarantee that your next session will be both inspiring *and* effective.

BEFORE

[1]
PRELIMINARY QUESTIONS

Understanding your audience and their needs is the key to success. Here are six questions to ask before your workshop:

- *What is the overall objective of the session?* Is your audience looking at a whole new brand positioning/business model, or is there a more specific aim such as new product development?

- *Who will attend?* The board will have a different perspective than the marketing department. The size of the group will also determine your approach.

- *Has your audience worked with trends before? If so, how and when?* This will help you gauge how much introductory "theory" and scene setting you will need.

- *What business challenge(s) does your audience face or see ahead?* Understanding these will enable you to choose the right trends and innovations to work with.

- *What trends is your audience already tapping into (or looking to)?* You can then cover these areas (or actively choose to

highlight what your audience *isn't* looking at).

- *How is the trend session integrated into other activities?* This is so that you can better understand your audience's frame of mind and goals.

[2]

WHEN TO USE
THE CANVAS

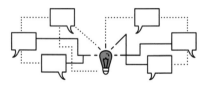

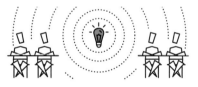

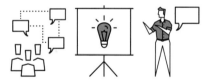

IDEATION AND BRAINSTORMING

Brainstorms are a great way to come up with novel ideas. But they can lack structure and focus. Participants struggle to develop and critique ideas constructively because they don't know how to dissect the underlying elements. The CTC gives participants a clear framework to follow.

STRATEGY BOOTCAMPS

Making plans about the future is exciting. However, strategy and tactics are too often driven by which resources the organization currently has available. Using the CTC ensures customers— the ultimate arbiters—aren't an afterthought.

NEW BUSINESS PITCHES

Using the CTC structures your approach. You will easily be able to communicate exactly where and how your proposals are grounded in customer needs, yet you are still well-positioned to take advantage of relevant external change and resolve meaningful tension.

[3]

SETTING UP
THE VENUE

If possible, hold the session off-site. Physical distance from "business as usual" will foster a mental distance that helps people be more creative.

Try to use a place that matches one of the trends you're looking at: a coworking space (if you're trying to understand disruptive startups), a private dining room of a restaurant (if you're focused on customer service innovation), or a gym (if you're trying to better understand health and wellness trends).

Arrive in good time to prepare. Don't be afraid to rearrange the space to foster collaboration and discussion. Try to have spaces without chairs and tables for the group work, hang posters on the walls, and encourage people to work while standing. They will be more active and more involved.

Lay out your materials. Check your presentation; use the clicker to run through the slides. Test the video and sound.

And of course, be on your toes for (the inevitable) last-minute technical or logistical issues!

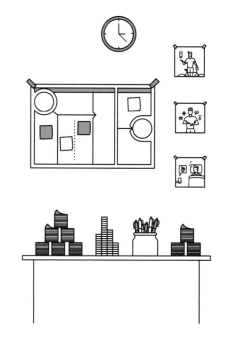

[4]
MATERIALS CHECKLIST

[TIP] Don't be a scrooge when it comes to stationery! You can never have too many props to trigger and capture people's ideas.

- ☐ Flipchart paper and poster-sized CTCs. Print them as big as you can!

- ☐ Sticky tack or tape: for hanging posters on the wall.

- ☐ Post-its (even better are Stattys): one pad per participant is a good rule of thumb.

- ☐ Markers: thick enough that they can be read from across the room!

- ☐ Supporting postcard-sized trend prompts:
  - · Trend definitions: Aim for 1-2 sentences.
  - · Key quotes, insights, or statistics.
  - · Real-world innovation examples (an image and short description).

- ☐ Clay or Legos to quickly model or prototype ideas.

- ☐ Dot stickers for voting on each others' ideas.

- ☐ Prizes for the winning group!

- ☐ Tech kit: laptop or tablet, adaptor to connect to the projector, USB memory stick, remote clicker.

- ☐ In the room: projector, sound, screen (remember to check in advance if it's 16:9 or 4:3 aspect).

DURING

Successful trend sessions
are inspiring, engaging,
relevant, and productive.
Here's how to deliver one.

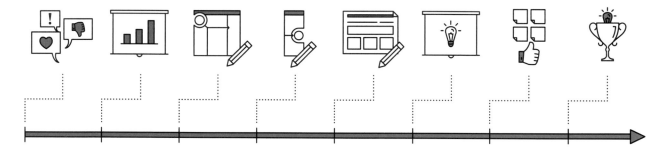

You've gotten everyone to carve out time in their schedules, the room is set up, and people are mentally primed to think beyond their day-to-day. Now you just need an agenda that will ensure people are creative yet focused. Here is ours.

We recommend spending at least half a day working through the steps covered in the following pages. Of course, it's great if you have longer and can dive deeper into people's ideas, and even start creating basic mock-ups and prototypes (see the next section—EXECUTE—for more on this). But three hours is about the minimum: taking in the warm-up, your trend presentation, a CTC group exercise, pitching back to the group, and your wrap-up.

[1]
START WITH WHY

Make sure you communicate the session's objectives clearly right at the start. Don't just focus on the "what." Start with "why." Why is it important that your audience gives everything during the session? Develop a sense of urgency, but one that's focused on opportunity. After all, trends are about uncovering exciting new opportunities and with them a brighter future. If possible, have someone senior reinforce the importance of a productive session, and remind people that their input matters.

[2]
PERSONAL DRIVERS

While the bigger picture (for the organization or, even bigger, for society) is important, it's also vital to motivate people on a personal level, too. Take five minutes at the start of the session to ask people to write down why they want to innovate. It could be because they want to make more money (for themselves or their families), to do meaningful work, to bring something new into the world, and more. Their answers don't have to be shared, but you can remind people to think back to their personal drivers throughout the day.

[3]

TREND PRESENTATON

Start your ideation sessions with an inspiring trend presentation to bring your audience instantly up to speed on the most relevant consumer trends and give them tangible examples of how others are already applying those trends. Present a mix of examples: not only from within your audience's industry and market, but also from outside in order to broaden their horizons and to inspire new thinking.

See Chapter 6 for a complete step-by-step guide to giving a compelling trend presentation.

[4]

CTC: GROUP EXERCISE

Next, have teams work through a trend from the presentation using the CTC (we covered how to do this in the previous chapter). If you have multiple groups, then everyone can either work with the same trend or different ones.

We recommend teams start with the left-hand side of the canvas (Analyze), ideally for at least 20 minutes. Then teams move on to the right-hand side (Apply), again for at least 20 minutes. The aim is to develop an innovation idea that will be pitched back to the group.

[5]
TEAM DESIGN

The teams you create should bring together people who don't normally work together. There are two benefits to this: first, diverse groups generate better ideas because people from different disciplines and backgrounds will have different perspectives and will make novel connections; second, involving people from across the organization will help secure a broad base of support and help when it comes to implementing ideas.

[6]
TEAM BUILDING

Before you start the group session, to ensure people are in the right frame of mind, let them take five minutes to chat informally. If people aren't familiar with each other (or are just nervous), then it can help to have some prompts. Project questions onto the screen such as:

- What's the one thing you can't live without (or what's the one thing your children can't live without, if you have them)?
- What are the best and worst brand experiences you've had recently?

- Which organization are you jealous of?
- Who is your "startup crush"?

These conversations will get them thinking about where and how their own expectations are being set.

[7]

MODERATING TEAMS

Every successful ideation session needs to have a strong moderator to steer the group and keep everyone on track. As the moderator, you are also responsible for creating an environment in which people feel comfortable sharing and presenting their ideas. Don't ever shoot someone's idea down in front of others or let anyone else do so!

Before starting the group exercise, be sure to remind people to:

- Listen
- Avoid dominance
- Evolve ideas, using phrases such as "yes and . . ."
- Ask open questions, such as: "Why is this happening?" "What does it mean?"

When teams are working through the CTC, you should circulate and remind people of these points and the overall objective of the session.

Don't let people be semi-present and absorbed in their phones. Create a digital detox station where people leave their phones, and give people time in between sessions to check in.

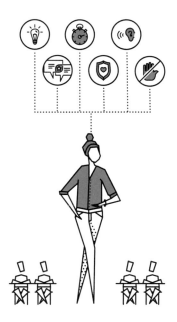

[8]
PITCHING TO THE GROUP

[9]
CHOOSING A WINNER

At the end of the group session, each team pitches their idea to the group. Set a countdown timer (90 seconds works well, certainly not more than 3 minutes). This keeps everyone's pitch focused and to the point.

Use the Innovation Worksheet to structure the presentation: name the innovation, describe it briefly, explain which type it is, which expectation it's catering to, and which customer segment it's aimed at. Try it yourself with the innovations in the previous chapter.

After the pitches, stick everyone's Innovation Worksheets on the wall. Give people stickers (dot stickers work well here) and have them vote for their favorite idea. Then add up all the stickers to see who won.

The winning team should then get a prize. This could be token (candy), more serious (a book or magazine subscription), fun (a day off), or something more material (a tablet or vacation voucher). One tip: always announce that there is a prize at the start of the session. It's amazing how it motivates people!

Head online to download an Innovation Worksheet.

TREND-DRIVEN IDEATION

AFTER

Here's how to end the session so it's not just a pleasant memory.

LEARNINGS

Before leaving the room, ask your audience to write down on a Post-it note the most important thing they learned during the session. Put them all up on the wall. Sharing these publicly will reinforce the learnings and inspire people.

FEEDBACK

To improve future sessions, ask the audience to leave (anonymous) comments about how the session could be improved.

IMPLEMENTATION ROAD MAP

Spend a few moments publicly outlining the next steps to progress with the winning idea (and perhaps any of the others, too!). What are the action points from the session, and more importantly, who will be responsible for getting the ball rolling on them?

TREND CHAMPION(S)

Ask for someone to volunteer to become your Trend Champion(s). They are then responsible for sharing updates on the trends worked with during the session.

FOLLOW-UP

Send participants digital copies of all the material presented and the tools they worked with during the session.

RECORD THE RESULTS

Take pictures of the completed tools – the Post-it Plus app is a great tool that digitizes your notes. And if you can leave the winning idea or some of the best posters up on the wall, do it! They may inspire others, too.

> NEXT

Having read this chapter, you now:

[1]   Know exactly how to run a successful ideation session with the Consumer Trend Canvas; and

[2]   Have a step-by-step workshop manual: pre-event questions, materials checklist, moderator's guide, tips on introducing a competitive element, and more.

Indeed, now that you've completed the GENERATE section of this book, you (and your team) are getting closer to being trend-driven innovators. There's one more hurdle to clear, however: that's the small matter of getting your new ideas into customers' hands.

....

Read the next section—EXECUTE—for a host of strategies you can use to take your new, trend-inspired innovation(s) to market.

....

EXECUTE

REALIZE YOUR IDEAS, OR REALIZE

THEY ARE USELESS

[EXECUTE]

So, you've unpacked a consumer trend with your team using the Consumer Trend Canvas, and you've ended up with a new innovation that will both reshape your existing customers' expectations and bring you countless new customers. Fantastic!

Now, how do you stop your shiny new idea from gathering dust or getting kicked to the curb by a skeptical committee? How do you bring it to life? How do you confirm it's worth doubling down on?

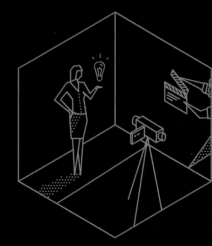

This section is designed to help you find the answers to those questions quickly, cheaply, and effectively, via half a dozen trend-based strategies that will get your idea out of a planning document and into customers' hands.

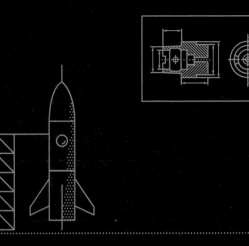

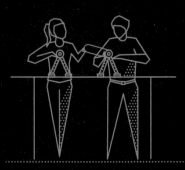
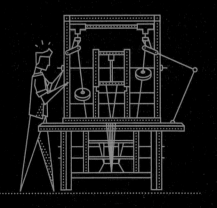

[5.1]

The First Yards

Make those initial

steps count.

THE FIRST YARDS

Make those initial
steps count.

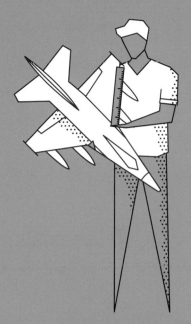

Despite all the pressure the Expectation Economy heaps on you, there's also never been a better time to be an innovator. Just as a host of macroforces—transparency, globalization, democratization, participation, personal expression, and more—have transformed *customers'* expectations, *organizations'* innovation capabilities have been radically enhanced as well.

The old world of innovation was characterized by its slow pace, high cost, and near-blind leaps of faith required when taking something to market. In contrast, the readily available, quick, and cheap approaches to building, testing, validating, and launching new innovations now mean that there is no excuse not to produce something that customers want.

Because we are trend *watchers*, we don't work with our clients to bring new ideas right through to market*. However, in the course of tracking emerging trends, we *do* see many of the same strategies being used again and again by successful innovators. Indeed, pop-ups and crowdfunding are customer trends themselves as well as launch strategies. Use the approaches featured in this chapter to inform and inspire *your* trend-driven innovation launches. Good luck!

There are many fantastic guides on how to successfully launch innovations. Find our favorites in the Further Reading section at the back of this book.

A QUICK NOTE ON RISK

Get your scrapbook of business book clichés ready!

Assuming this isn't your first innovation rodeo, you'll have seen plenty of ideas that some higher-up has deemed too risky or unsubstantiated, whether it was an emailed photo of a scrawl on the back of a napkin or a robust and detailed strategy your team conceived during a weeklong offsite meeting. Even if you are the CEO or work alone, you may have had friends, peers, family, or your own inner skeptic shooting down an idea, highlighting everything that might go wrong or the challenges you will face.

Yet the business truism is, of course, absolutely true: "If something is completely risk-free, it is no longer an opportunity." Don't worry. We don't expect you to give a coffee mug emblazoned with that quote to your CFO (although that would be awesome). However, to delight customers and surpass their expectations, you (and your CFO) must accept a certain level of risk.

Trend-driven innovation does not, unfortunately, eliminate uncertainty (see the Failure Gallery in Chapter 2 for a raft of on-trend ideas that didn't quite work out). There are still endless hurdles to be overcome: production, distribution, marketing, and many more.

However, if you've followed the methodology this far, your ideas will at the very least be deeply anchored in core consumer needs, inspired by businesses that are already raising expectations, and primed to capitalize on change, rather than hide from it.

Let's look at half a dozen routes to market that will inspire your launch strategies.

VAPORWARE

Test demand with
virtual proof-of-
concepts.

Of all the new strategies featured in this chapter, this one is perhaps the hardest for many professionals to get their heads around, as it involves going to real customers, not just focus groups with products that don't exist. Yet.

Vaporware is a computing term that refers to products that are announced but never actually manufactured. Now we're obviously not suggesting you intentionally mislead customers. However, it's never been easier to create supporting material for a planned new product or business concept, thereby allowing you to gauge the reaction before deciding whether to proceed.

One of the quickest and easiest approaches is to invest $100 into online advertising. Make your pitch. Do people click on the ad? If not, then perhaps the point of tension you are resolving is less acute than you expected. Go one step further and create a splash page detailing your upcoming product, and ask people to sign up to be notified when it launches. Do they?

Alternatively, virtual prototypes are almost free to create and share with the world. Take advantage of this and pull together a beautiful video mockup of your new concept. Once you release the video, you'll soon discover whether it excites people, as the two examples opposite discovered in spectacular fashion.

KUAISOU CHOPSTICKS

"SMART" PRODUCT SPOOF FINDS
FAVOR WITH CHINESE CUSTOMERS

Chinese web giant Baidu originally released a video about its contamination-sensing "smart chopsticks" as an April Fool's prank. However, the video struck a chord with food safety-conscious Chinese viewers who had been burned by multiple recent food scandals. Indeed, the video created so much excitement that the company developed a working prototype, which Robin Li, the company's CEO, presented at the Baidu 2014 World Conference. The Kuaisou chopsticks can test the pH levels of drinking water and detect recycled cooking oil—known locally as "gutter oil"—by monitoring TPMs (total polar materials), which indicate freshness. Data is relayed to an app for instant results.

PHONEBLOKS

DESIGNER'S CONCEPT BECAME A
GOOGLE-SUPPORTED REALITY

Dutch designer Dave Hakkens developed Phonebloks, a concept for a modular smartphone, which can be upgraded with new components to reduce e-waste. After creating a video detailing the concept, he turned to "crowdspeaking" site Thunderclap—where supporters "donate" social media posts, rather than money—aiming to attract 500 supporters. Within a month, over 900,000 people had pledged their support. Motorola then announced it would work with the Phoneblok community on Project Ara, its open-source, modular phone effort. In early 2015, Google (which acquired the Project Ara team) announced the modular Spiral 2 phone would be piloted in Puerto Rico.

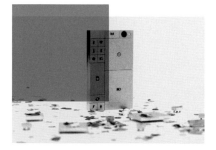

HACK DAYS

Use trends to power a hackathon.

The first recorded "hackathon" took place in 1999, when 10 programmers gathered in Alberta to work on the OpenBSD operating system. Since then, the practice of bringing people together for a day, night, or weekend to focus intensely on a specific theme or problem has turned into a phenomenon, with events hosted by students, cities, agencies, corporates, nonprofits, governments, and more. The Facebook "Like" button was invented at an internal hackathon. British Airways organized a hackathon on a flight from San Francisco to London in 2013. Guns N' Roses guitarist Slash organized a "slashathon" to ask fans to think about how he could promote his new album.

Indeed, hackathons are no longer only attended by software developers, but now often simply aim to bring people together to ignite creative approaches and fast-paced problem solving. Consumer trends provide the perfect fuel (along with coffee and pizza!) for generating ideas that are focused on solving people's problems.

Before hosting a trend-driven hackathon, use the Consumer Trend Radar to determine which trends relate to the hackathon's overarching objective. If you already know the trends you want to work with, you can kick off the day with a Consumer Trend Canvas ideation session—as Alfa-Bank did opposite—before moving on to the protyping and pitching phases.

[CASE STUDY]
ALFA-BANK

42 Agency, a Moscow-based advertising agency; and Alfa-Bank, the largest privately owned bank in Russia, organized a 24-hour trend-powered hackathon in 2014 that led to the launch of a novel bank account product.

At the start, participants were presented with several consumer trends, including CURRENCIES OF CHANGE. As we saw in the previous section, in this trend people are incentivized to achieve their personal goals (such as exercising more) with increasingly innovative,

fun, and ultimately relevant rewards. They then unpacked these using the Consumer Trend Canvas.

Combining the emerging customer expectations around relevance and personalization with their knowledge of Russian consumers, one team developed a concept for a new type of bank account. They pitched an app-based system that syncs with fitness trackers to allow customers to benefit financially from exercising—by having money moved into an account with a higher rate of interest.

The idea was launched to the public just one and a half months after the hackathon, as "Alfa Activity." Customers can connect their wearable fitness tracker (such as FitBit, Jawbone UP, or RunKeeper) to their bank account, and as in the original concept, every step taken sees money transferred from their checking account into a special savings account paying a higher interest rate than is otherwise publicly available.

Alfa-Bank reported that by December 2014 (nine months after launch), more than 1 million kilometers had been tracked by Alfa Activity customers, who were saving at twice the rate of the bank's average customers, and exercising 1.5 times more than the average Moscow resident. A win-win all round!

PROTOTYPING

Get making!

As with business plans, no innovation idea survives its first contact with people. Building a prototype will bring your idea to life and allow you to start collecting that all-important feedback.

There are two types of prototype you should be aiming to create—even by the end of your ideation session or hackathon—internal proof of concept/demonstrations or more advanced customer-facing, at least semi-functional products.

Internal concepts are great at building support for your idea.

They can be totally virtual (as basic as mocked-up diagrams in Keynote), or physically built (use clay, Legos, or cardboard). These early models will obviously require people to look beyond their current form, but putting *something* in people's hands to tinker and play with will get their minds to open up to the possibilities.

Remember to follow design agency IDEO's advice when prototyping, and present colleagues or clients with multiple prototypes. Having two or more versions spurs

discussion and avoids "take-it-or-leave-it" decisions.

Also, push yourself to think beyond building just conceptual models. Prototyping can—and for digital services, increasingly should— also extend to launching actual customer-facing, functional models that will test and validate customer demand, the holy grail when launching new ideas.

Mint Digital, a digital and product development agency based in London and New York, runs an annual hackathon and prototyping program they call "Four Days to Launch" (4D2L), where they aim to conceive and birth entire new business ventures. By the final day, if not before, teams need to have an operational business (not just virtual mockups). At the very least, the new businesses should have genuine users, with revenues if not actual profits the real goal!

Indeed, the company has used rapid prototyping and hackathons to launch a number of side projects cum minibusinesses recently. One such project is DeskBeers, a subscription service delivering local craft beers to office workers on Friday afternoons. Strong demand saw it spun out as an independent company, raising approximately $175,000 in equity crowdfunding in January 2015.

You might not plan to start a whole new venture, but it *is* a powerful challenge: could you create and attract customers to a new business in a matter of weeks or even days?

POP-UP PROOF

Versatile. Affordable.
Exciting.

Since we first coined the phase "pop-up retail" in 2004, the trend (and customers' love for it) has shown no sign of abating.*

Refer back to the core elements of trends, and it's easy to see why pop-ups resonate with customers. They tap into the basic desire for novelty and excitement, while the shift toward even-greater abundance means that it's hard for people to know what to pay attention to. At the same time, pop-ups subvert the expectation that everything will be always available as and when needed and, as such, demand customers' attention.

Pop-ups also work for businesses. Their limited scope makes them fertile testing ground for your trend-driven initiatives. Pop-ups are affordable, they can be deployed almost anywhere (from shipping containers to subway stations), and they allow you to try new and creative concepts.

Indeed, pop-ups aren't limited to simply being retail outlets. You can launch almost any idea as a pop-up experience: create a space where customers can interact with your new offering, give away free samples, teach people how to use a new product, gather feedback, and more.

---

* Indeed, this is why we struggle to give a definitive answer when people ask us how long trends will last. Many wrote off the pop-up trend as a frivolous fad, good only for marketing stunts. Yet even if the novelty of the concept itself has worn off, well-executed experiences continue to delight, even when fleeting.

THE GUARDIAN

FROM SMALL TO LARGE SPACES

The U.K. newspaper opened a pop-up coffee shop, #guardiancoffee, in London's BOXPARK (itself a pop-up mall of shipping containers—how meta) as part of its "open journalism" initiative. Following the initiative, the newspaper announced the development of the Midlands Goods Shed, a 30,000-square-foot space that will become an event space and, of course, a coffee shop.

IKEA

TRIALING WITH TRAVELERS

IKEA has run a number of novel pop-ups in Paris, including creating an open access lounge at the Roissy-Charles de Gaulle airport, which included beds for passengers to lie on. This followed the installation of a 54-square-foot "apartment" inside the city's Auber metro station, where six people lived for five days in order to promote its new range of space-saving furniture.

WARBY PARKER

CLICKS-TO-YURTS-TO-BRICKS

Much has been made of Warby Parker's transformation from online eyewear e-tailer to a retailer claiming sales per square foot second only to Apple. Yet it wasn't a blind leap. Before launching its first physical store in 2013, Warby Parker's founders ran makeshift shops in their apartment, their office, and multiple pop-ups (including a repurposed old school bus and a yurt in a SoHo garage!).

PRE-TAIL

Validate and build a
customer base even
before launch.

In 2014, people pledged over $1,000 a minute to as-yet-unrealized projects on Kickstarter alone. For customers, the attractions of crowdfunding platforms are obvious: a sense of connection with the project's creator, being ahead of the mainstream, access to exclusive perks, and the thrill of finding a truly exciting or useful or relevant product. Indeed, we've already touched on how these crowdfunding PRE-TAIL platforms help drive the Expectation Economy forward (see Chapter 1).

But crowdfunding gets even more interesting when we look at the opportunities it presents to trend-driven innovators. Finally, you have a method of assessing genuine customer demand by confirming whether customers will actually go all the way to entering their credit card details and commit to purchasing your upcoming product.

That's not to say that crowdfunding is the easy option. Far from it. Exposing your product to the crowd requires a level of transparency and communication for which you need to prepare meticulously. But done well, it can be a great route to building an early and evangelistic customer base. That's why big brands are now joining garage entrepreneurs in pursuing PRE-TAIL launch strategies. However, existing resources and bigger budgets should make crowdfunding a strategy that is more about generating excitement rather than sharing risk. The idea is to make early purchasers feel like partners, not suckers.

[CASE STUDY]
SONY

In November 2014, the minimalist e-ink FES Watch raised over $23,000 in its three-week campaign on the Japanese crowdfunding site Makuake (beating its target of $17,000). Fashion Entertainments, the project's creator, then revealed it was in fact part of electronics giant Sony. The brand announced that it had released the watch under a pseudonym in order "to test the real value of the product." Following this, Sony then launched its Qrio Smartlock—a connected lock that enables the owner to open their door with their smartphone and share virtual entry "keys" via social apps—on the same site. The project was also successfully funded, raising over $200,000. Kunitake Saso, a customer insight specialist involved with both projects, explained that "crowdfunding platforms offer a chance to quickly see how users engage with a new product and to better understand the potential of the idea before launching it. This process allows Sony to act like a nimble entrepreneur."

NO BUDGET, NO PROBLEM

Learn from these ultra-affordable, trend-driven innovations.

PRIX DU CAFÉ EN TERRASSE

UN CAFÉ : ....7€

UN CAFÉ, S'IL VOUS PLAIT." ....4,25€

"BONJOUR, UN CAFÉ, S'IL VOUS PLAIT."1,40€

Nothing can be more frustrating than identifying an unmet customer expectation and generating a compelling idea to meet it, only to be told there is no budget available. However, subscribe to the notion that trend-driven innovation is about resolving points of customer tension, and it becomes clear that your innovations don't have to cost a fortune. Doing something for and with customers that doesn't cost much is a powerful way to signal to colleagues that trend-driven innovation is within reach.

Indeed, on-trend innovations need not involve expensive new technologies, rolling out an entirely new product line, expanding to far-flung markets, or buying airtime during the Super Bowl.

Concepts that delight customers can often be dirt cheap to roll out, as the handful of our favorite low- to no-budget innovations opposite show. What cheap but cheerful innovations can *you* come up with?

LA PETITE SYRAH

A café in France implemented a daring pricing policy based on customers' politeness. People who greeted the barista warmly and said "please" were charged €1.40 for their coffee; those who failed to use any pleasantries were penalized and charged €7. The prices (with greeting) were clearly displayed on a chalkboard inside the cafe.

LIBÉLULA BRECHÓ

A vintage store in Curitiba, Brazil, launched a very simple campaign to enable people to donate clothing to the homeless at the start of winter. Hangers were placed on trees around the city and people were encouraged to leave items for homeless people to take away.

VODACOM

When South African telecoms operator Vodacom's network failed, CEO Pieter Uys took to Twitter to address critics directly. He apologized personally for the issues and assured customers that the company was addressing them. Uys continued tweeting until the problem was fixed.

COFFEE JOULIES

After complaints that U.S. manufacturing meant high prices for the company's metal "beans" that keep coffee at a drinkable temperature for longer, the founders set up an online vote. Two coupons were available to customers: a $5 "USA" coupon, or a $10 "China" coupon (to reflect the lower cost of offshore manufacturing). The majority of customers went for the larger discount, and Coffee Joulies are still made in New York State.

> NEXT

Having read this chapter, you now:

[1] Have half a dozen proven strategies to launch your trend-driven innovation(s) quickly, cheaply, *and* effectively;

[2] Know how to obtain genuine customer feedback on new ideas; and

[3] Are about to merely skim the rest of the book because you can't wait to get going!

However, while executing a single idea is a great start, in the Expectation Economy, this will be but a momentary advantage.

....

In order to see sustained success, you'll need to build a CULTURE of trend-driven innovation. The next section will show you how.

....

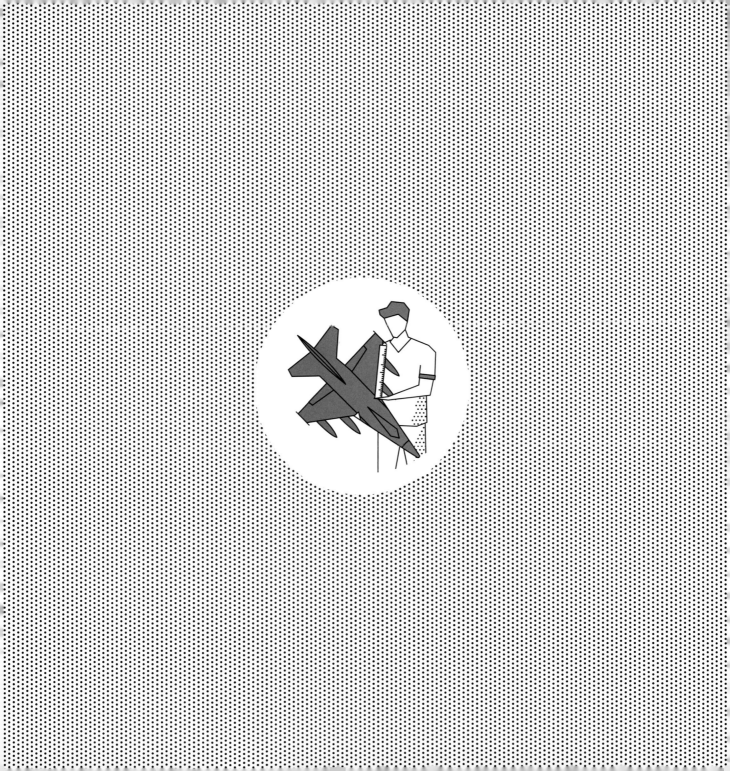

CULTURE

UNLOCK AN OPPORTUNITY MACHINE

[CULTURE]

Successful organizations don't win by spotting a single trend, no matter how big or game-changing it is. From ever-present behemoths such as General Electric to recently emerging giants such as Google, organizations succeed by recognizing and acting on multiple trends, in ways small and large, time and again. In short, they win because they *build a trend-driven culture* that can sense the direction of travel of customer expectations on an ongoing basis.

This section will show you how to kickstart and develop trend-based initiatives within your own organization, and how to leverage the power of external networks, too.

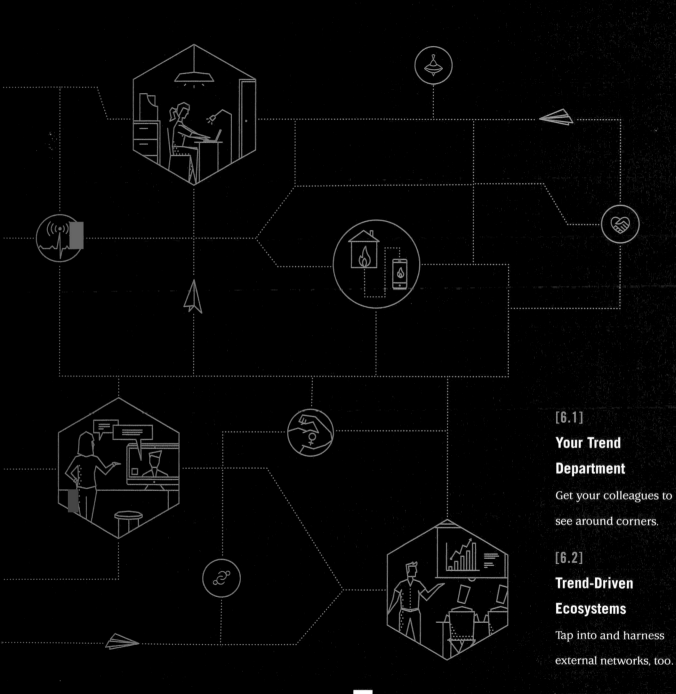

[6.1]

Your Trend Department

Get your colleagues to see around corners.

[6.2]

Trend-Driven Ecosystems

Tap into and harness external networks, too.

YOUR TREND DEPARTMENT

Get your colleagues to see around corners.

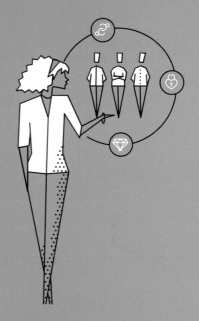

The most powerful cultural dimension of a trend-driven organization is its inclusiveness. Which tells you—though you've probably realized already—that the idea of a "Trend Department" is a misnomer: Trend watching shouldn't be limited to a select few within your business. To stay ahead of accelerating customer expectations, everyone in your organization should be a trend watcher: empathetic to people's needs, alert to moments of tension, and aware of the opportunities that will come from resolving them.

As this book has shown, there's no mystique to spotting trends (despite what umpteen "gurus" would have you believe). Most people don't think about trends because they don't know what they are looking for, not because they are unable to. Yet people are innately attuned to spotting the places where tension and opportunities are emerging. Unmet expectations lie beneath people's statements of frustration with the products they use on a daily basis, such as "I can't understand why . . .?" and "Why can't I . . .?"

Certainly, your customer service team will know what expectations you face as a business, as they will regularly hear what your customers expect to be able to do with your products!

This chapter will show how to strengthen the trend muscles in your organization by stimulating, unlocking, and harnessing the natural insights and impulses relating to customer expectations that your team have inside themselves.

INSPIRE

Give a trend presentation your audience can't stop thinking about.

There are few better ways to kickstart your trend-driven innovation efforts than with a trend presentation. It sets the agenda, shows people what you mean by trends, and most importantly communicates the value placed on trend-driven innovation.

That being the case, you had better make sure that your next trend presentation is a good one. We've given hundreds of trend presentations over the past decade to audiences of all descriptions. Here's how we structure them.

WHEN AND WHY?

Trend presentations are a great addition to company town hall meetings, strategy and planning sessions, inspiration sessions and away days, project kickoffs, lunch and learn events, and more.

But ultimately, wherever and whenever you deliver it, your trend presentation should *inspire* your audience to take immediate action and *empower* them to spot upcoming future trends themselves.

People should leave the session with no doubt that trends aren't just "nice to know" or "interesting," but contain actionable insights that they *need* to deploy, and soon. You should constantly challenge people to not just understand a trend, but think how they will apply it to their vision, business model, products, and marketing campaigns.

TREND-DRIVEN INNOVATION

BUILDING THE PERFECT TREND PRESENTATION

The detailed step-by-step guide.

[1] OVERALL STRUCTURE

Of course, your presentation's structure will depend on its purpose, but there are a few we use again and again:

- The Future of X: 3-10 trends relevant to your industry, company, or market.
- 3-4 key mega-trends: with each big theme illustrated by an actionable, relevant, "smaller" emerging trend.
- Mega-trend deep dive: 3-4 trends that illustrate the future direction(s) of a single big idea.

[2] TREND SELECTION

As well as using the Consumer Trend Radar (see FOCUS), you can select relevant trends by working:

- Top-down: from the company mission statement, strategy, or project objective.
- Bottom-up: analyze a selection of recent innovations in a region or industry, and present the trends they relate to.
- Outside-in: proactively present trends other sectors or markets are experiencing, in order to provoke new perspectives.

[3] **TREND NARRATIVE**

Each trend you present should tell a compelling "story:"

- Open with an intriguing trend name to arouse curiosity. Remember FLAWSOME?
- What basic human need does the trend satisfy? What are the key drivers of change that make the trend relevant right *now*?
- Present supporting data and statistics to keep the left-brained members of the audience happy. Rapid movements or surprising data points work best.
- Show 3-6 innovations that illustrate the trend. Ask people to consider which new customer expectations these will create.
- Close with a "lightbulb moment." Challenge people to think about how to adapt the examples and apply the trend for their customers.

[4] **INNOVATION SELECTION**

Which innovations to include? Again, the examples you show should tell a story:

- Open with a well-known (if slightly older) example to orientate the audience. The examples that follow will then show how the trend is evolving.
- Feature at least one example that saw unarguable success, such as crazily large sales or download numbers, to hit home the reality and impact of the trend.
- Use examples from a wide range of industries and markets, especially less obvious ones, to show people the breadth and consistent presence of the underlying customer expectation.
- Choose at least one example that the audience can experience for themselves. This could be via video or, if a digital innovation, prompt them to visit the site or download the app.
- Make sure to include an example from your audience's market/sector, to show that their peers are *already* acting on the trend.
- Feature a very novel or cutting-edge example, and use it to demonstrate where the trend—and customer expectation—is headed in the future.

Head online to download a trend presentation template.

INFORM

Share the information
that matters, in ways
that inspire.

Giving a trend presentation is just one way to get people up to speed. Strongly customer-focused cultures don't just look at what is happening at the annual strategy session. They establish regular practices that help them continually sense the direction in which customer expectations are headed.

Indeed, simply by finding ways to make people more aware of game-changing innovations (and talking about the trends that underpin them), you'll inspire a culture where people start to think about trends and also where new opportunities to delight customers might lie.

There are endless ways to disseminate trend information around your team. Try creating an internal newsletter; create innovation screensavers to display on screens in your office; use social networks (see the case study on the PHD Source platform); put up physical posters. Or get physical, as in the KILN IdeaKeg case study opposite. Some of our clients even hang trend posters in the washroom!

[CASE STUDY]
KILN IDEAKEG

While virtual information is easy, quick, and cheap to share, encouraging people to get hands-on with trend-based innovations is a great way to ensure that the underlying insights really resonate and develop.

One of our favorite approaches to disseminating trend information is innovation advisory boutique KILN's IdeaKeg. Subscribers receive regular deliveries of a box containing seven "cultural artifacts," each one illustrating an emerging trend. For example, objects have included seed "bombs" (that can be "planted" by throwing onto overlooked urban areas), tea in silk tea bags, Sugru putty that can be used to repair household objects, and a keyless padlock.

The boxes are designed to be used in a workshop setting. Objects are accompanied by a short summary of the underlying trend, while a facilitator's manual suggests questions to ask about each object. These help participants assess the objects and connect them to the challenges the business faces.

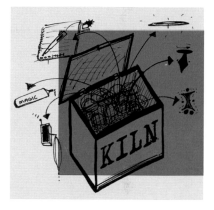

As Kate Hammer, KILN's cofounder and "commercial storyteller" says, "If you only tell people things, their minds draw a blank. When you create an environment where people can ask questions, creative thinking comes alive. Trends are a trigger to get people to ask better questions."

COLLABORATION

Many minds make
light work.

Successful trend-driven cultures do more than just share information; they share *ideas about how to act on that information*.

Just as our approach to trend watching encourages you to use innovations to tap into the collective intelligence of the business crowd, you should also ensure that your internal approach to trend analysis is equally diverse. Varied perspectives and inputs all increase the potential that you will make the novel connections that others are less likely to spot.

It's not always easy to encourage your team to share their insights on the innovations they see changing customer expectations and suggest ways your organization can respond. Most people are (rightly) focused on successful execution in their daily activities, not innovation. However, a culture of trend-driven collaboration will ultimately make your team's work lives more meaningful, enjoyable, and effective, as PHD's Source platform opposite shows.

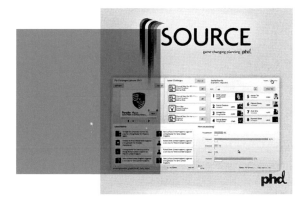

[CASE STUDY]
PHD SOURCE

One of the challenges identified by global media and communications agency PHD was how to service and manage multinational client accounts while remaining agile and innovative.

Its solution was to create an internal online collaboration platform Source, as a place to conceive, design, and implement the media planning and buying strategies for its clients—and to not only involve staff assigned to those specific clients, but anyone in the entire company.

To encourage contributions, the agency introduced a gamification element. People receive "pings" for each action they take on the system, whether that be suggesting a new idea or helping to advance or optimize an existing one. Public leaderboards allow employees to see how their contributions rank relative to others (for the past day, week, month, and year; on a local and global level). These encourage usually friendly competition between the various participants and offices. There are annual awards for leading

employees, although these focus on intrinsic peer recognition rather than tangible rewards such as cash prizes.

Incredibly, after three months of full deployment, 75 percent of PHD's 3,000 staff were using the platform, 1,500 doing so daily. The agency attributed the input from a diverse range of local offices as being critical in winning a $3 billion Unilever global account.

TRAINING

Create a crack team
of trend-driven
innovators.

Clearly your team is not going
to become expert and active
practitioners of trend-driven
innovation overnight. It takes time
and commitment to ensure that
a culture takes root—and while
presentations, workshops, away
days, and other one-off activities
help, they will not be enough in
isolation.

Training programs are a powerful
way of signaling to employees that
trend-driven innovation is a priority
for your organization. They're
also a great staff retention tool

if they deliver meaningful value
and development to individual
participants. Here are two
innovative innovation (!) training
programs worth learning from:

[1] THNK AND VODAFONE

The Vodafone Navigator program,
launched in spring 2015, saw the
telecoms giant partner with THNK
School of Creative Leadership.

The custom program was
designed around applying THNK's
four innovation steps—sensing,
visioning, prototyping, and

scaling—to a real-life business
issue facing Vodafone Netherlands.
To that end, participants came
together for four two-day modules
over a six-month period to learn the
process behind creative thinking.

Vodafone executives not only
developed their innovation skills
during the six-month program, they
also solved a material business
issue facing the company. As a
result, the program's return on
investment was quickly quantifiable
in terms of business performance
indicators.

[2] STRATEGYZER

Strategyzer is a business software and online training company set up by the team behind the Business Model Canvas, a popular one-page framework for analyzing business models that inspired our own Consumer Trend Canvas.

Tim Murphy, then chief product officer at MasterCard, engaged Strategyzer to deliver a training program that covered both the Business Model Canvas and Value Proposition Design (the follow-up framework).

One of the key objectives of the program was to enable colleagues to have better conversations around new ideas by giving them a set of tools, frameworks, and most importantly, what Strategyzer's cofounder Alexander Osterwalder calls "a shared language with which to discuss innovation and value creation" (from the perspective of both the business and customers).

The pilot started in late 2013, when training was initially delivered in-person to the executive team, and to team members globally via an online course that combined self-directed learning and live remote video classroom sessions.

Following positive feedback from participants, the program had been taken by 10 percent of the global workforce and 50 percent of the product team after one year, with the tools now forming part of the formal process of innovation planning and assessment within MasterCard.

EMPOWER

Unleash staff to
conceive innovations
of their own.

Inspiration, training, and discussion mean nothing if you don't also establish a culture that both encourages and actively enables people to practice trend-driven innovation for themselves.

In a perfect world, organizations would be filled with people who spontaneously spot, suggest, design, and implement new innovations, and have the processes in place that allow them to do so. However, the very focus and structure that allow consistently successful execution at scale in most companies (especially larger ones) means that innovations spawned during "business as usual" moments will often be limited to sustaining or incremental ones at best.

Yet the relentless forces of creative destruction mean that every organization *must* also seek to generate truly novel or even disruptive innovations (however much of an overused business cliché that concept is now!).

One compelling way to do this is to initiate specific programs or competitions where staff can propose, pitch, and ultimately launch new innovations themselves. The organizational benefits are many: intense bursts of focus and excitement, a sense of recognition and engagement, and diverse perspectives on where new opportunities lie.

[CASE STUDY 1]

MONDELEZ
FLY GARAGE

Snack brand Mondelez launched its Fly Garage innovation incubator initiative in Argentina in 2012. The now five-day program (each iteration has seen this reduced from its original three-week length) brings Mondelez employees together with agencies +Castro and Contagious, entrepreneurs, students, and external "agitators" to inspire innovative digital experiences.

The process contains three stages: creation, prototyping, implementation. Interestingly, participants are introduced purely as individuals; their positions are not disclosed to reduce preconceptions. Teams rotate every three hours during the idea generation phase so there are no owners of an idea. Maria Mujica, Mondelez's Latin American marketing director and Fly Garage lead, observes: "the garage is like a social smoothie, with trends an essential ingredient. To innovate, we expand our perspectives by going out of our category, and without trends we cannot start."

To ensure buy-in at the implementation stage, senior executives outline the overall strategic themes in advance; however, teams are encouraged to explore a broad spectrum of consumer culture and trends to generate project briefs.

After rapid prototyping, the brand looks to implement the ideas with the most potential. One such initiative was Beldent's Random Fest, a music festival with four stages centered around a lighthouse, which took place in 2013. Each artist would play three tracks, before the lighthouse would randomly shine its light to announce which band would play next. The show was attended by 10,000 fans and streamed to a further 250,000 people online.

[CASE STUDY 2]
ADOBE KICKBOX

Adobe VP of Creativity Mark Randall heard employees cite the same obstacles preventing them from being innovative: no time alongside their day job, difficulty in securing resources, and lack of clarity about how to launch ideas.

As a result, the company launched its Kickbox initiative to address these head-on. Any employee can request a Kickbox and managers cannot veto a request. They receive a physical red box containing an innovation "toolkit:" a chocolate bar, a $10 Starbucks card, Post-It notes, a notebook, a step-by-step innovation manual and, most importantly, a prepaid credit card with $1,000.

Participants are challenged to work through six stages (Inception, Ideate, Improve, Investigate, Iterate, Infiltrate). During the Ideation stage, participants are instructed to scan trend websites as one of the "external sources [that] are essential to spark new observations and questions about the world."

If participants complete the final stage and successfully present their tested and validated idea to executives, they receive a follow-up blue box with additional resources and guidance to continue its development.

Participants reported that the prepaid credit card (No receipts required! No approvals!) suddenly transformed the company's talk of innovation from a management cliché into something that employees were being trusted—expected, even—to deliver.

In January 2015, Adobe released the program and supporting materials to the public, enabling anyone to download and access the materials for free.

Your idea could
travel the world

[CASE STUDY 3]
AVIVA
CUSTOMER CUP

Multinational insurance company Aviva launched its Customer Cup competition in 2008; since then over 1,300 internal teams have participated.

The competition encourages any employee to submit an idea via the company's idea management system. Richard Wilkinson, Customer Cup innovation manager, says: "Trends are stimuli for idea generation. They offer context and insight that helps people focus upon developments which are desirable for our customers and business." Colleagues can comment and vote on submissions, which encourages people to build support among their peers.

Local CEOs select promising ideas, and around 100 are advanced to the semifinals. At this stage, proposers have to recruit five additional people to form a small team, develop the idea further, and submit a business case. A judging panel then selects 10 entries to progress to the three-day Grand Final, held at a prestigious venue where teams present their final pitch to members of Aviva's group executive.

Andrew Brem, Aviva's chief digital officer, estimates that the competition has generated nearly £75 million in net benefits to the company to date.

YOUR TREND DEPARTMENT

LABS

Separate,
accommodate, and
experiment.

Another method of encouraging and supporting trend-driven innovation within larger organizations is to create separate, specific units that have innovation as their ongoing focus and are explicitly positioned as labs, skunkworks, or similar. Being separated from the core—and granted a mission of creative destruction—enables these units to experiment with, execute, and deploy new ideas at a faster pace than the corporate structure allows but at that which customers and the market demand.

Labs also make sense for customers, whose expectations toward national and multinational corporations are stratospheric and unremitting; indeed, if a major retailer releases a new service and it breaks or flounders, the backlash *will* be public and immediate. Setting up a lab unit allows organizations to deliver new products and services to early adopters in a (very slightly) less pressured environment.

Labs are not a quick win, though. You need strong executive commitment, and half-baked attempts to inject "startup thinking" and agility into a lumbering parent organization will fail.

However, when done right, labs can help attract and retain inventive, ambitious people who wouldn't tolerate working in a more confined corporate setting, as well as helping you produce the meaningful, trend-driven innovations that offer new opportunities to delight customers.

[CASE STUDY 1]

@WALMARTLABS: SAVINGS CATCHER

[CASE STUDY 2]

WESTFIELD: DINE ON TIME

Founded in 2011 after the world's largest retailer acquired online search and discovery platform Kosmix, @WalmartLabs employs over 3,500 people (not your average lab!).

One project is Savings Catcher, released in March 2014. Shoppers scan their Walmart receipts with the smartphone app, which then checks if local competitors offer any of the purchased products for less. If the app finds lower prices, the difference is automatically refunded within 72 hours onto a Walmart gift card. The retailer reported in September 2014 that it had returned $2 million to customers via the app.

Mall operator Westfield established its San Francisco-based lab in 2012. The 70-person division is headed by Kevin McKenzie, the company's global chief digital officer, and targets innovation at the convergence of digital and real-world retail.

One of the projects piloted by the lab is a food-ordering app, Dine on Time. Users can preorder food from restaurants in the Westfield San Francisco Center to avoid waiting in line, or arrange to have meals delivered to their home or office. Users can also use the app to order off-menu special dishes.

> NEXT

Having read this chapter, you now:

[1] Can deliver a killer trend presentation and inspire your team;

[2] Know the main activities a trend department should be focused on; and

[3] Have seen some real-world examples of how other organizations are conducting trend-focused activities.

....

Next, learn how to extend these outside the boundaries of your organization in order to tap into the wider ecosystem of ideas, inspiration, and opportunities.

....

TREND-DRIVEN ECOSYSTEMS

Tap into—and harness—external networks, too.

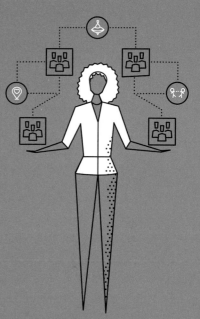

The accelerating pace of change means that even the most attuned of organizations can't hope to keep up by relying purely on its own resources. As Sun Microsystems cofounder Bill Joy observed: "It's better to create an ecology that gets all the world's smartest people toiling in your garden for your goals. If you rely solely on your own employees, you'll never solve all your customers' needs."

And just as organizations with an effective *internal* trend-driven culture follow certain similar patterns of activity, we have found that organizations with strong *external* cultures consistently participate in and support certain activities, too.

This chapter analyzes the most powerful methods that companies like Unilever, GE, Barclays, Telefónica, and others use to connect, challenge, and work with outside actors, and shows how you can use these strategies to stay ahead of customer expectations.

At first glance, the activities in this chapter appear focused on larger companies. However, they are just as relevant to smaller companies, too. Indeed, large companies often seek to engage with smaller startups in their attempts to foster trend-driven innovation.

Wherever you sit, this chapter should give you ideas as to how to connect with those on the "other side" and unlock growth.

NETWORK

Building connections beyond your walls.

The last chapter looked at how sharing information among the members of your team is critical to obtaining a better understanding of trends. In the same way, sharing information and learning from those who are not part of your organization allows you to benefit from others' experiences and insights.

Indeed, the idea of a porous network of external collaborators is central to how we operate at TrendWatching. Our free trend publications give us a platform from which we recruit trend spotters to TW:IN (TrendWatching's Insight Network). We rely on this network of passionate trend enthusiasts to help inform us about new innovations and the direction of customer expectation. Once we spot a potential new or evolving trend, we turn to the network with questions: are similar innovations happening in their markets and industries? Does it have broad appeal?

Digital technologies offer organizations an incredible ability to build and engage with communities on a global scale at low cost. These can be organized around a theme (such as consumer trends) or even around a specific trend, as Crowd Companies (opposite) is.

Whichever is the case, being part of a vibrant network enables you to benefit from a diversity of opinion, experience, and insight that your internal resources can't match.

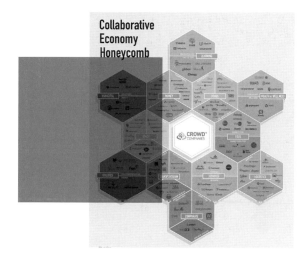

Collaborative Economy Honeycomb

[CASE STUDY]
CROWD COMPANIES

Crowd Companies is a network with a mission "to bring Empowered People & Resilient Brands together to collaborate for Shared Value." It was founded in late 2013 by ex-Forrester social media analyst Jeremiah Owyang, to reflect his view that the Collaborative Economy represented a more meaningful and long-lasting trend than social media. The network connects large companies with the disruptive startups active in shaping the Collaborative Economy and has three main activities:

[1] **Brand council**: to enable corporate members (typically chief innovation officers) to share experiences and challenges with their peers at private physical events and via an online platform.

[2] **Educational services**: to give members the chance to learn from startup practitioners and access research data on the Collaborative Economy.

[3] **Partnering**: to bring both sides of the network (corporate and startup) together to explore new business opportunities.

Founder corporate members included Barclaycard, Ford, GE, Nestle, and Walmart, and membership doubled in the first year to 48 companies across a range of industries. Collaborative Economy innovator members include crowdfunding platform IndieGogo, makerspace TechShop, ridesharing platform Lyft, and job marketplace Elance-oDesk.

CROWD-POWERED INNOVATION

The best minds don't work for you.

The notion that no matter how large or compelling your organization is, most of the smartest people will still be working for someone else is what underpins "open innovation," a term coined by Haas Business School professor Henry Chesbrough in 2003.

Open innovation encompasses many concepts and approaches, but the central idea is that companies need to seek external inputs when innovating in order to source new ideas and to deliver novel solutions.

Certainly, the past decade has seen profound changes in both companies' mind-sets and abilities in this area, and a 2014 Haas Business School study showed that 78 percent of large companies were now engaged in some form of open innovation.

Typical open innovation approaches include:

[a] **Competitions**: contests can engage diverse crowds to solve problems, often with fresh perspectives and in a fraction of the time and cost of internal efforts.

[b] **Communities**: the open source software movement is a great example of where an "unmanaged" crowd community can outperform directed, top-down efforts.

[c] **Platforms**: technological APIs that enable data to be integrated into third-party services, while managed platforms such as mobile app stores allow third parties to extend or build on core functionality.

[CASE STUDY]
EYEKA AND UNILEVER

eYeka is a global crowdsourcing platform founded in France in 2006 that connects brands and creatives through online challenges.

The platform now has over 300,000 registered creatives from over 150 countries. They have submitted over 85,000 ideas in response to the 750 brand challenges posted, in return for over €5 million in prize money. Challenges typically target product development and design, brand positioning, and specific campaign ideas for consumer product brands.

A powerful example of an open creative process can be shown by Unilever's "Dirt Is Good" 2012 challenge. The global campaign was designed to reassure mothers that allowing their children to play in less than totally sanitized environments is beneficial to their personal development.

The monthlong contest saw 88 ideas submitted from 29 countries, with the most coming from France, China, Indonesia, Russia, and India. However, the winning idea was a 3D animation submitted by

a German dancer, which was then adapted into a TV commercial for Unilever's Breeze Active Bleach in the Philippines. The global brain indeed!

Other brands that have used the platform include dental care brand Oral B (which sourced ideas for a connected brushing app), Citroën (which sourced designs for personalization options for their DS3 model), and Carrefour (which sourced concepts for its campaign celebrating 20 years since it entered the Turkish market).

TREND-DRIVEN ECOSYSTEMS

HOUSE

Share physical space
to get exposure to new,
on-trend ideas.

Despite the digitalization of so much of our daily lives and the ability the online world offers organizations to tap into external networks as we've seen, the power of physical proximity and interaction remains strong.

One thing that larger, incumbent organizations frequently have is a surplus of physical space, or at the very least, the resources to provide space. Sharing space with smaller startups, creative communities, and even individuals can lead to a sharing of ideas and development

of trend-driven initiatives that may otherwise never be considered.

On the demand side, the changes in working habits and resources required to start a business mean that entrepreneurs and small teams can come together quickly to test an idea. Indeed, since the term was first used by freelance product engineer Brad Neuberg in San Francisco in 2005, coworking spaces have exploded in popularity, roughly doubling every year to an estimated 2,150 spaces globally at the end of 2012. Many of these

are now provided or sponsored by corporates, with the Hatch example opposite showing how these spaces can even be created from underutilized corporate assets.

However, while coworking spaces and coffee shops are suitable for those who simply need a laptop to advance their ideas, innovators who require more heavy duty hardware will be willing audiences for organizations who can offer them physical space and exposure to such equipment—as in the case of GE's Garage initiative, opposite.

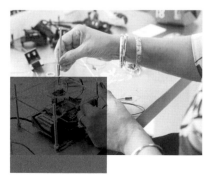

[CASE STUDY 1]

BARCLAYS: HATCH

As part of its efforts to support entrepreneurs and small businesses, financial services giant Barclays has launched a number of space-based initiatives. In addition to opening traditional coworking spaces in London and Manchester, the bank partnered with nonprofit 3Space in late 2014 to open "Hatch," a coworking space focused on social enterprises and community groups, in a vacant ex-Barclays bank branch in Oxford. Qualifying users can use the coworking space for free, while the unit also hosts mentoring sessions and a makerspace with sewing machines, workshop tools, and access to a 3D printer.

[CASE STUDY 2]

GE: GARAGE

Over the past decade conglomerate GE has made building a strong externally focused innovation culture a strategic priority. Its Garage project started in early 2012 in Austin, Texas, with an objective to stimulate interest in domestic manufacturing and invention. Garages are GE-funded makerspaces where people can come to learn about and use advanced manufacturing hardware, including laser cutters, 3D printers, injection molders, and Arduino kits. In 2014, GE launched a global tour, establishing pop-up Garage spaces in Lagos and Algiers, and in 2015 visited Brussels and Berlin.

VENTURING AND ACCELERATION

If you can't beat them, fund and scale them!

The final alternative method of building a strong external trend-driven culture, for larger incumbent companies especially, is to invest directly in the very startups that threaten to disrupt them. Indeed, the growing awareness of the threat from new startups has driven a doubling of corporate venturing units in five years to 1,100.

These larger companies are well aware that they might struggle to meet emerging customer expectations as quickly as newer organizations. However, the hope is that they *can* invest in, work with, and even help scale those companies that otherwise might threaten them.

Especially in the nondigital world, where production and distribution at scale pose serious operational challenges, partnering in some form or other can be very attractive for smaller organizations. Even startups with a digital product can often be seduced by the resources and large existing customer bases of incumbents, as Telefónica's Wayra program (opposite) shows.

However, as we saw in the introduction, venturing and acceleration is no silver bullet, not when smaller and newer organizations enjoy many advantages, both in terms of their agility and responsiveness, but also because as CLEAN SLATE BRANDS, they are often perceived by customers to be more ethical and trustworthy.

The reality is that, as always, finding the right partner is critical—for both sides.

[CASE STUDY]
TELEFONICA WAYRA

Facebook's $19 billion purchase of WhatsApp, the messaging service that at the time had only 55 employees yet served over 450 million monthly users, symbolizes the severe threat of disruption facing incumbent telecommunication providers.

In response, multinational provider Telefónica has established a wide-ranging open innovation program. It includes Wayra, a startup accelerator program that launched in Latin America and Spain in 2011. By early 2015, the program had expanded to 14 "Wayra Academies" in 12 countries, including Argentina, Brazil, Mexico, Colombia, Germany, and the U.K.

Successful startups sell between 7 and 10 percent equity to Telefónica in return for up to $50,000 in cash funding and the same amount in services. Startups get housed for six months in a physical Wayra coworking space; they gain access to Telefónica's technological expertise and to executives to whom they can pitch their products and services. After six months, the startups have to move out of the physical spaces and seek additional funding.

By 2015, the program had received nearly 30,000 applications, with 438 being accepted. Telefónica reported that 61 percent had gone on to receive an additional $99 million in funding from third-party investors, while 80 companies also piloted or trialed projects with the core Telefónica business.

> **NEXT**

Having read this chapter, you now:

[1] Understand the opportunities that reaching beyond the limits of your organization can unlock; and

[2] Have witnessed a number of examples of practical initiatives you can pursue.

A culture of trend-driven innovation is one that allows you to build and leverage both internal and external resources. Critically, this turns trend-driven innovation from a one-off activity into an ongoing process, and one that will keep you ahead of customers' accelerating expectations.

....

This brings us almost to the end of our guide to trend-driven innovation. Turn over for a final wrap-up and summary of the end-to-end journey!

....

OVER TO YOU . . .

The examples featured in this book are truly just a tiny snapshot of the astonishing creativity and unprecedented choice that characterize the world we now live in. There are over 1.4 million apps in the Apple App Store alone, and 2014 saw over 1,000 apps added every day. More than 300 hours of video are uploaded to YouTube every minute. Amazon.com added more than 20 million items to the site in the first nine months of 2014, taking its product selection to over 250 million items.

While the competition for customers' attention is extreme, the opportunities for those that win customers' hearts and minds—and wallets—are just as mind-boggling. Facebook's recent acquisitions show how quickly value can be created: paying $1 billion for Instagram 18 months after it launched, $2 billion for Oculus Rift less than two years after its successful crowdfunding campaign, and $20 billion for five-year-old WhatsApp. Xiaomi, now the world's third-largest smartphone maker after Samsung and Apple, is valued at $46 billion. It released its first phone in 2011. After five years of operations, Uber is facilitating over 1 million rides a day in more than 300 cities worldwide. And it's not just hot mobile and technology startups that are growing exponentially; consumer and retail brands applying to the equity crowdfunding platform CircleUp have an average annual growth rate of 93 percent.

You picked up this book because you want to build things that people love. We hope that the trend-driven innovation methodology both inspires and empowers you. Yes, much hard work lies ahead. Spotting trends, figuring out which ones offer the most compelling opportunities, designing and launching brilliant new concepts—these are not easy tasks. However, standing still is not an option.

Following the trend-driven innovation playbook will ensure that your next customer-centered initiative is successful, but more importantly it will help you build an organization that sees success again and again. And alongside the professional and financial rewards, practicing trend-driven innovation—making things that matter to people—is intensely personally rewarding. Catering to people's most fundamental human needs and desires, making their lives better, creating a better future for all of us—who doesn't want to be a part of that?

So, what next? This book is just the start of your trend journey. Analyze and learn from the 40 trends and

BRING IT ALL TOGETHER AND CREATE THE NEXT BIG TREND.

over 100 featured case studies. Use the tools and strategies to launch winning innovations of your own. Develop a mind-set and a culture that anticipates what customers will want next. Bring it all together and *create* the next big trend.

We will be watching!

FURTHER READING

CONSUMERISM AND BRANDING

Seth Godin, *Tribes: We Need You to Lead Us* (Portfolio, 2008)

Umair Haque, *The New Capitalist Manifesto: Building a Disruptively Better Business* (Harvard Business Review Press, 2011)

Joseph Heath, Andrew Potter, *Nation of Rebels: Why Counterculture Became Consumer Culture* (Harper Business, 2004)

Martin Lindstrom, *Buyology: Truth and Lies About Why We Buy* (Doubleday Business, 2008)

Grant McCracken, *Chief Culture Officer: How to Create a Living, Breathing Corporation* (Basic Books, 2009)

Debbie Millman, *Brand Thinking and Other Noble Pursuits* (Allworth Press, 2011)

Marty Neumeier, *Zag: The Number One Strategy of High-Performance Brands* (New Riders, 2006)

Clotaire Rapaille, *The Culture Code: An Ingenious Way to Understand Why People Around the World Buy and Live as They Do* (Broadway Books, 2008)

Rob Walker, *Buying In: The Secret Dialogue Between What We Buy and Who We Are* (Random House, 2008)

TRENDS

Malcolm Gladwell, *The Tipping Point: How Little Things Can Make a Big Difference* (Abacus, 2002)

Chip and Dan Heath, *Made to Stick: Why Some Ideas Survive and Others Die* (Random House, 2007)

Kevin Kelly, *What Technology Wants* (Penguin Books, 2011)

Mark Penn, E. Kinney Zalesne, *Microtrends: The Small Forces Behind Tomorrow's Big Changes* (Twelve, 2007)

Martin Raymond, *Trend Forecaster's Handbook* (Laurence King Publishing, 2010)

Everett M. Rogers, *Diffusion of Innovations, 5th edition* (Free Press, 2003)

Nassim Nicholas Taleb, *The Black Swan: Second Edition: The Impact of the Highly Improbable* (Random House Trade Paperbacks, 2010)

Henrik Vejlgaard, *Anatomy of a Trend* (Confetti Publishing Inc., 2012)

INNOVATION

Scott Anthony, *The First Mile: A Launch Manual for Getting Great Ideas into the Market* (Harvard Business Review Press, 2014)

Clayton M. Christensen, *The Innovator's Dilemma: The Revolutionary Book That Will Change the Way You Do Business* (HarperBusiness, 1997)

Nathan Furr, Jeff Dyer, *The Innovator's Method: Bringing the Lean Startup into Your Organization* (Harvard Business Review Press, 2014)

Frans Johansson, *The Medici Effect: What You Can Learn from Elephants and Epidemics* (Harvard Business Review Press, 2004)

Steven Johnson, *Where Good Ideas Come From* (Penguin Books, 2010)

Larry Keeley, Helen Walters, Ryan Pikkel, Brian Quinn, *Ten Types of Innovation: The Discipline of Building Breakthroughs* (Wiley, 2013)

Alexander Osterwalder, Yves Pigneur, *Business Model Generation* (Wiley, 2010)

Alexander Osterwalder, Yves Pigneur, Greg Bernarda, Alan Smith, *Value Proposition Design* (Wiley, 2014)

Eric Ries, *The Lean Startup: How Today's Entrepreneurs Use Continuous Innovation to Create Radically Successful Businesses* (Crown Business, 2011)

Marc Stickdorn, Jakob Schneider, *This Is Service Design Thinking: Basics, Tools, Cases* (Wiley, 2012)

BUSINESS

Chris Anderson, *The Long Tail: Why the Future of Business Is Selling Less of More* (Hyperion, 2006)

Larry Downes, Paul Nunes, *Big Bang Disruption: Strategy in the Age of Devastating Innovation* (Portfolio, 2014)

Thomas Friedman, *The World Is Flat: A Brief History of the Globalised World in the Twenty-First Century* (Allen Lane, 2005)

Lisa Gansky, *The Mesh: Why the Future of Business Is Sharing* (Penguin, 2010)

Salim Ismail, Michael S. Malone, Yuri van Geest, *Exponential Organizations: Why New Organizations Are Ten Times Better, Faster, and Cheaper Than Yours* (Diversion Books, 2014)

Marc Levinson, *The Box: How the Shipping Container Made the World Smaller and the World Economy Bigger* (Princeton University Press, 2006)

Christian Madsbjerg, Mikkel Rasmussen, *The Moment of Clarity: Using the Human Sciences to Solve Your Toughest Business Problems* (Harvard Business Review Press, 2014)

Idris Moote, *Design Thinking for Strategic Innovation: What They Can't Teach You at Business or Design School* (Wiley, 2015)

Ernst Schumacher, *Small Is Beautiful: A Study of Economics As If People Mattered* (Vintage, 1973)

Clay Shirky, *Here Comes Everybody: The Power of Organizing without Organizations* (Penguin Books, 2009)

IDEATION AND PRESENTATIONS

Nancy Duarte, *Resonate: Present Visual Stories That Transform Audiences* (Wiley 2010)

Dave Gray, Sunni Brown, James Macanufo, *Gamestorming: A Playbook for Innovators, Rulebreakers and Changemakers* (O'Reilly, 2010)

Frederik Härén, *The Idea Book* (Interesting, 2004)

Bryan W. Mattimore, *Idea Stormers: How to Lead and Inspire Creative Breakthroughs* (Jossey-Bass, 2012)

Jon Steel, *Perfect Pitch: The Art of Selling Ideas and Winning New Business* (Wiley 2006)

NOTES AND SOURCES

WHY NOW

[1.1] **Welcome to the Expectation Economy**

For more on companies featured in the Global Snapshot: GrabTaxi http://grabtaxi.com/, Sol de Janeiro's skin cancer initiative: https://www.youtube.com/watch?v=VKzliSgq0Yg Nrml, Headphones: https://www.nrml.com/

Amazon's best-selling and most reviewed shredder: http://www.amazon.com/AmazonBasics-12-Sheet-Cross-Cut-Credit-Shredder

More on Domino's turnaround: http://www.businessinsider.com/dominos-turnaround-story-2014-10?IR=T while the quote is taken from a session by Domino's CEO at Michigan's Grand Valley State University: http://www.mlive.com/business/west-michigan/index.ssf/2015/02/dominos_ceo_doyle_talks_super.html

World Intellectual Property Indicators 2014 edition: http://www.wipo.int/ipstats/en/wipi/

Uber's blogpost about spiraling expectations: http://blog.uber.com/eta-expectations

Read more about the crowdfunding projects mentioned: https://kickstarter.com/projects/597507018/pebble-e-paper-watch-for-iphone-and-android, https://kickstarter.com/projects/1523379957/oculus-rift-step-into-the-game, https://kickstarter.com/year/2014

Tesla strong sales reported: http://ww11.jato.com/PressReleases/Strong%20demand%20in%20the%20EU%20%E2%80%98Big%205%E2%80%99%20markets%20drives%20September%20growth%20in%20European%20new%20car%20sales.pdf

Patagonia's "Don't Buy This Jacket" campaign email: http://www.patagonia.com/email/11/112811.html and background on $20 Million & Change and other initiatives: http://www.bloomberg.com/bw/articles/2013-05-06/patagonias-latest-product-an-in-house-venture-fund

Lockitron's DIY crowdfunding story: http://techcrunch.com/2012/10/07/the-story-of-lockitron-crowdfunding-without-kickstarter/

Stephan Olander's quote is taken from his session at Cannes Lions advertising festival: http://www.adweek.com/news/advertising-branding/how-nike-made-just-do-it-obsolete-141252

Flow Hive crowdfunding page and full story: https://www.indiegogo.com/projects/flow-hive-honey-on-tap-directly-from-your-beehive, watch a video about Brahma Seleção Especial: https://www.youtube.com/watch?v=yD8QljwZ55U, W Hotels defending its wedding social media concierge: http://www.fastcompany.com/3028261/fast-feed/w-hotels-defends-its-3000-social-media-wedding-concierge-to-some-this-may-seem-a-b after it was publicly criticized on Twitter: https://twitter.com/bbosker/statuses/448468488898637824

Read more about Selfridges' various initiatives: http://www.selfridges.com/en/info/aboutMuseumOfEverything/, http://www.selfridges.com/content/article/bompas-parr%E2%80%99s-rooftop-crazy-golf-selfridges-london, http://www.selfridges.com/content/article/festival-of-imagination-london, http://www.selfridges.com/content/article/everyman-cinema-booking

Warren Buffett quote: http://eu.wiley.com/WileyCDA/Section/id-817935.html

Airbnb's growth: http://marketwired.com/press-release/airbnb-celebrates-record-growth-with-10-million-guest-nights-booked-1670787.htm

Background on BlaBlaCar's trust and motivation survey: http://magazine.ouishare.net/2013/01/blablacar-online-trust-study/, data on the fundraising initiative: http://techcrunch.com/2014/07/01/blablacar-raises-a-massive-100-million-round-to-create-a-global-ride-sharing-network/

SCAN

[2.1] Trends 101

Tinder's usage stats: http://www.nytimes.com/2014/10/30/fashion/tinder-the-fast-growing-dating-app-taps-an-age-old-truth.html

Listen to Daniel Ek, Spotify's founder talking about his experiences with Napster: http://pando.com/2012/11/08/how-napster-gave-birth-to-spotify/

[2.2] Watch businesses first, customers second

Read our BRAND SACRIFICE trend featuring these bets on the future: http://trendwatching.com/trends/brand-sacrifice/

Jeffrey Hollender explained the history of Seventh Generation in a personal interview. Read more about Sustain at: http://www.forbes.com/sites/susanadams/2014/06/13/sustainability-and-marketing-to-women-comes-to-condoms/

Steve Jobs quote from Walter Isaacson, *Steve Jobs: The Exclusive Biography* (Little, Brown, 2013)

Marriott & GoPro initiative: http://news.marriott.com/2015/01/gopro-marriott.html

Miya's Sushi: http://miyassushi.com/invasive-species-menu/

Honest By's transparency policy: http://www.honestby.com/en/news/147/100-transparent.html

Project Ara: http://projectara.com/

Airbnb's Happy New Year video: https://www.youtube.com/watch?v=5yDQIhrX5_0, its interactive real-time map of travel activity: https://airbnb.com/map

Webvan's bankruptcy: http://news.cnet.com/Webvan-delivers-its-last-word-Bankruptcy/2100-1017_3-269594.html vs. Ocado's share price history: http://www.ocadogroup.com/investors/share-price-centre.aspx

The rise and fall of Myspace: http://www.bloomberg.com/bw/magazine/content/11_27/b4235053917570.htm

http://mashable.com/2006/07/11/ myspace-americas-number-one vs. Facebook's user statistics: http:// newsroom.fb.com/company-info/

Burger King's scaling back of Satisfries: http://fortune.com/2014/08/13/so-long-satisfries/ vs. Lyfe Kitchen's expansion detailed at: http://lyfekitchen.com/in-the-news/

Mattel's Shanghai closure: http://www .bbc.co.uk/news/business-12670950 vs. its repositioning: http://www.forbes .com/sites/helenwang/2013/11/17/can-mattel-make-a-comeback-in-china/

Car2Go U.K. withdrawal: http:// www.bbc.co.uk/news/uk-england-birmingham-27546644 vs. its broader success: http://europe.autonews.com/ article/20141113/ANE/141119923/ car2go-poised-to-top-1-million-users and DriveNow's London launch: http:// www.ft.com/cms/s/0/755e72bc-7899-11e4-a33c-00144feabdc0.html

Starbucks' mobile payment success vs. Google's: http://www.wired .com/2014/11/forget-apple-pay-master-mobile-payments-starbucks/

[2.3] Trends in the wild

Nest Protect: https://nest.com/smoke-co-alarm/life-with-nest-protect/

Riddell Insite Impact Response: http:// www.riddell.com/InSite

Ford concept smart seat: http://www .fordmediacenter.nl/persberichten/587/ documents/safe_ecg_seat_EU1515.pdf

Baidu's smart chopsticks: https://www .techinasia.com/baidu-smart-chopsticks-detect-dodgy-cooking-oil/

Getty Image's Lean In collection: http:// www.gettyimages.co.uk/collections/ leanin

Pantene's Labels Against Women campaign: https://www.youtube.com/ watch?v=-K2kfgW7708

Lady Mechanic Initiative: http:// ladymechanicinitiative.org/graduation-of-25-female-mechanics-in-benin/

IAmElemental action figures: http:// www.iamelemental.com/

Behind the scenes at a McDonald's photo shoot: https://www.youtube.com/ watch?v=oSd0keSj2W8

Pink goop in Chicken McNuggets? McDonald's Canada answers: https://www.youtube.com/ watch?v=Ua5PaSqKD6k

View third-party reviews on Four Seasons site: http://fourseasons.com/ newyork/

Kysy Vaikka: http://www.if.fi/web/fi/

henkiloasiakkaat/vahingot/kysy-vaikka/ pages/default.aspx

House of Masaba: http://www .perniaspopupshop.com/designers/ masaba#

Botanique opening: http://www .luxurytravelmagazine.com/news-articles/botanique-hotel-spa-exclusive-new-hotel-opening-in-brazil-17991.php

Avi Arad's *The Rise of the Terracotta Warriors*: http://usa.chinadaily.com.cn/ epaper/2013-08-29/content_16929439 .htm

Muhtesem Yüzyıl (Magnificent Century): http://www.reuters.com/ article/2012/12/14/rohde-turkey-idUSL1E8NE4A920121214

Budweiser's Chinese New Year campaign: http://adage.com/article/ global-news/budweiser-greet-chinese-year-times-square/239661/

FOCUS

[3.1] Post-Demographic Consumerism

For more on Harley-Davidson catering to women: http://www.bloomberg.com/ bw/articles/2014-06-02/can-harley-davidson-finally-woo-women.

Attitudes of Malaysian youth to tradition—from the Young & Rubicam

Generation Asia survey 2014, read more here: http://www.thestar.com.my/Business/Business-News/2015/01/03/A-touch-of-culture-Brands-can-leverage-on-Asians-desire-to-preserve-identity/?style=biz

Mobile shoppers by age: http://nielsen.com/us/en/insights/news/2013/who-is-the-mobile-shopper-.html

Overlap between the lists of 1,000 favorite music artists across the generations: http://www.theguardian.com/media/2014/may/25/radio-1-playlist-secrets-uncovered-battle-of-brands

Increase in the number of female video gamers over 50: http://www.theesa.com/wp-content/uploads/2014/10/ESA_EF_2014.pdf

Chinese citizens using social media: http://us.kantar.com/media/908826/0202-en-infographic-1950.pdf

Male opinion of grooming products in Asia: http://www.kantarworldpanel.com/id/News/kwp-asian-men

Over 65s using social media: http://www.pewinternet.org/data-trend/social-media/social-media-use-by-age-group/

Increase in mixed-race marriages: http://www.aacap.org/AACAP/Families_and_Youth/Facts_for_Families/Facts_for_Families_Pages/Multiracial_Children_71.aspx

DDP Yoga: https://ddpyoga.com/ and read more at: http://www.nytimes.com/2014/08/17/magazine/the-rise-of-beefcake-yoga.html

Wayung Kulit with *Star Wars* characters: https://www.facebook.com/peperanganbintang

Moët & Chandon vending machine in Selfridges: http://www.harpersbazaar.co.uk/fashion/fashion-news/moet-and-chandon-champagne-vending-machine-selfridges

Phil Schiller tweets 1 billion iOS devices sold: https://twitter.com/pschiller/status/560197288048340992

Uniqlo revenues to February 2015: http://www.fastretailing.com/eng/ir/news/1504091800.html and read more about the Uniqlo ethos: http://uniqlo.com/us/company/about-uniqlo.html

Facebook monthly active users: http://newsroom.fb.com/company-info/

Bülent Arinc's speech and the Twitter reaction: http://www.bbc.co.uk/news/blogs-trending-28548179

Choose from 1,000 kinds of Nike shoes: http://store.nike.com/gb/en_gb/pw/shoes/brk

The US Environmental Agency on bottled water: http://www.ct.gov/dph/lib/dph/environmental_health/pdf/05_frequently_asked_questions_about_bottled_water.pdf

Estimate of products for sale on Amazon: http://export-x.com/2014/08/14/many-products-amazon-sell-2/

The British Medical Journal studies the Ice Bucket Challenge: http://www.bmj.com/content/349/bmj.g7185

Wall Street Journal poll on gay marriage: http://blogs.wsj.com/washwire/2015/03/09/support-for-gay-marriage-hits-all-time-high-wsjnbc-news-poll/

South China Morning Post on China's rising divorce rate: http://www.scmp.com/news/china/article/1535515/heartbreaking-news-nations-divorce-rate-rises-13-cent

Coca-Cola's America the Beautiful campaign: http://www.coca-colacompany.com/stories/america-is-beautiful-and-coca-cola-is-for-everyone

Banco do Brasil: http://www.bb.com.br/

Tanishq Wedding Film: https://www.youtube.com/watch?v=P76E6b7SQs8

Harley-Davidson tree pledge: http://www.harley-davidson.com/content/h-d/en_US/company/renew-the-ride.html

Moët Hennessy launch Indian wines: http://www.bbc.co.uk/news/business-25326578

Versace M.I.A.x Versus collection: http://www.versusversace.com/collections/mia

Lululemon's yoga store for men: http://time.com/3584541/lululemons-men-store-soho/

The LG Wine smartphone: http://www.lgwinesmart.co.kr/

Thug Kitchen vegan blog: http://www.thugkitchen.com/

Zappos explains its PinPointing service: http://blogs.zappos.com/blogs/technology/2012/08/29/introducing-pinpointing

Barclaycard Bespoke Offers: http://www.barclaycard.co.uk/business/bespoke-offers

The All Things Hair YouTube channel: https://www.youtube.com/user/AllThingsHairUK

[3.2] Evaluating Trends for Opportunity

Read more about Professor C Bodin, the first female LEGO scientist:

http://abcnews.go.com/blogs/lifestyle/2013/09/lego-unveils-first-female-lego-scientist/

More on Itaú Unibanco's initiative for female entrepreneurs: http://www.redemulherempreendedora.com.br/noticias/geral/itau-mulher-empreendedora

Walmart announces its "Women Owned" initiative: http://news.walmart.com/news-archive/2015/03/11/walmart-launches-women-owned-logo-in-store-online

The Diffusion of Innovations by Everett Rogers: http://www.amazon.com/Diffusion-Innovations-5th-Everett-Rogers/dp/0743222091

Big Bang Disruption by Larry Downes and Paul Nunes: http://www.amazon.com/Big-Bang-Disruption-Devastating-Innovation/dp/1591846900

What'sApp user base: WhatsApp hits 700 million monthly active users in 2015: https://gigaom.com/2015/01/06/whatsapp-hits-700-million-monthly-active-users/

The Rise and Fall of Draw Something: http://www.forbes.com/sites/insertcoin/2012/05/04/draw-something-loses-5m-users-a-month-after-zynga-purchase/

Tinder market share graph from 7Park data, see more here: http://uk.businessinsider.com/tinder-plus-being-tested-in-europe-2015-2

Quotes from Jeffrey Hollender sourced during conversations and email correspondence in March and April 2015.

More on Target pop-ups, including that 2002 pop-up on the Hudson River: http://www.bloomberg.com/apps/s?pid=newsarchive&sid=aZf1Jgg78pyk

Nike's pop-up in SoHo for the Knicks game: http://www.nytimes.com/2006/11/16/nyregion/16lebron.html?_r=0

H&M Scheveningen resort pop-up: http://inhabitat.com/hm-starts-the-summer-right-with-a-pop-up-container-store-on-the-beach/

YrStore pop-up: https://www.wearepopup.com/p/yrstore/

Target Too pop-up exhibition: http://www.brandchannel.com/home/post/2015/03/27/150327-Target-Too.aspx

Himmat emergency alert app: https://play.google.com/store/apps/details?id=com.smartcloud.delhi&hl=en

China survival guide app: https://itunes

.apple.com/cn/app/zhong-guo-qiu-sheng-shou-ce/id527824265?mt=8
Mercedes cloud computing data privacy service: http://www.bloomberg.com/news/articles/2014-09-18/mercedes-sets-up-cloud-firewall-to-halt-car-data-hacking
Lumkani slum fire detector: http://lumkani.com/
UNICEF Proteja Brasil app: http://www.protejabrasil.com.br/br/

Kenco Coffee vs Gangs: https://www.coffeevsgangs.com/
Whisper Touch the Pickle ad: https://www.youtube.com/watch?v=5s8SD83ILJY
JP Morgan Chase invest in Detroit: http://www.jpmorganchase.com/corporate/Corporate-Responsibility/detroit.htm
Botafogo and Puma inverted stripes campaign: https://vimeo.com/97000647
BrewDog anti-Putin beer: https://www.brewdog.com/lowdown/blog/hello-my-name-is-vladimir

[3.3] The Consumer Trend Radar

Michael Porter as quoted in *Fast Company*: http://www.fastcompany.com/42485/michael-porters-big-ideas

Read more about BMW DriveNow:

http://www.drive-now.com
Read more about Audi Unite: https://www.audiunite.com/

Cuervo History in a Bottle app: https://itunes.apple.com/gb/app/cuervo-history-in-a-bottle/id850755840?mt=8
Normal 3D-printed earphones: https://www.nrml.com/
Malaysian IKEA fans dress as their favorite product: http://designtaxi.com/news/369038/IKEA-Fans-Dress-Up-As-Their-Favorite-Product-From-The-Brand-To-Win-Contest/

Starbucks app "order ahead" function: http://www.bloomberg.com/news/articles/2014-10-16/starbucks-to-test-order-ahead-mobile-app-in-portland-area
Skol Consulado campaign: http://www.skol.com.br/consulado/
Grabble: https://www.grabble.com/

GENERATE

[4.1] The Consumer Trend Canvas

The Footprint Chronicles: https://www.patagonia.com/us/footprint
The Invasive Species Menu at Miya's Sushi: http://miyassushi.com/invasive-species-menu/
Tesla's record-breaking sales in

Norway: http://www.hegnar.no/motor/artikkel496745.ece

Read more on CLEAN SLATE BRANDS here: http://trendwatching.com/trends/cleanslatebrands/
TOMS "One for One" model: http://www.toms.com/improving-lives

Value Proposition Design: https://strategyzer.com/value-proposition-design

[4.2] The Consumer Trend Canvas in Action

Read more on SYMPATHETIC PRICING here: http://trendwatching.com/trends/sympathetic-pricing/
Havas' Meaningful Brands Index from June 2013: http://www.havasmedia.com/press/press-releases/2013/meaningful_brands_beat_stock_market

South China Morning Post's coverage of Occupy Central: http://www.scmp.com/topics/occupy-central
Uber's Boston bus strike promotion: http://blog.uber.com/BPSfreerides, #keeplondonmoving promotion: http://blog.uber.com/tubestrike
See a video about BGH's "My Home Is An Oven" campaign: https://vimeo.com/94715375

HarvardX and MITx joint study on Open Online Courses from January 2014: http://papers.ssrn.com/sol3/papers .cfm?abstract_id=2381263

GOQii homepage: http://us.goqii.com
Codementor: https://codementor.io/
Rise: https://rise.us

See more on BRANDED GOVERNMENT here: http://trendwatching.com/ trends/10-trends-for-2015/#slide-21

Havas Worldwide's Prosumer Report on "Communities and Citizenship" (January 2013) contains more on consumers expecting businesses to step in where governments fail: http://www .prosumer-report.com/blog/wp-content/ uploads/downloads/2013/01/prosumer-communities-and-citizenship.pdf

Dial Direct's Pothole Brigade disbands: http://leadsa.co.za/?p=8507
Clean Romania: http://cif.ro/despre
Embajada Zona 18: http:// embajadazona18.org

PersonalHeroes: http://personal-heroes .com
Read more on CURRENCIES OF CHANGE here: http://trendwatching .com/trends/currencies-of-change/

We spoke with Stephie Knopel, founder of PersonalHeroes, about how she used the Consumer Trend Canvas to develop a concept.
The Havas Worldwide's Prosumer Report on "Communities and Citizenship" (January 2013) contains more on how millennials expect to use social media for good: http://www .prosumer-report.com/blog/wp-content/ uploads/downloads/2013/01/prosumer-communities-and-citizenship.pdf
Klout: https://klout.com
Happify: http://www.happify.com
Spire: https://spire.io

EXECUTE

[5.1] **The First Yards**

Baidu's smart chopsticks: https://www .techinasia.com/baidu-smart-chopsticks-detect-dodgy-cooking-oil/
Find the latest news from the Phonebloks community here: https:// phonebloks.com

For more about the evolution of hackathons: http://www.ft.com/ cms/s/0/88212d8a-a716-11e4-8a71-00144feab7de.html

We spoke with Nikolai Khlopov, managing partner at 42 Agency, on how they used a trend-powered hackathon to develop Alfa-Bank's Activity account: http://activity.alfabank.ru/Activity

We spoke with Tim Morgan, director of Mint Ventures at Mint Digital, about the 4 Days To Launch rapid prototyping process; find more here: http://4d2l .mintdigital.com
DeskBeers' equity crowdfunding page: https://www.crowdcube.com/ investment/deskbeers-17148

Take a trip all the way back to 2004 for the first of many Trend Briefings we have written on POP-UP RETAIL: http:// trendwatching.com/trends/POPUP_ RETAIL.htm

#guardiancoffee: http://www.thedrum .com/stuff/2013/05/30/guardian-announces-launch-guardiancoffee-shoreditch, The Midland Goods Shed: http://www.theguardian.com/ membership/midland-goods-shed-progress/2014/sep/10/-sp-midland-goods-shed-guardian-events-membership-building-space
IKEA in Paris: http://www.nydailynews .com/life-style/real-estate/ikea-home-home-paris-airport-article-1.1114043
Warby Parker's SoHo yurt: http://www .nytimes.com/2012/01/05/fashion/

warby-parkers-pop-up-store-offers-eyeglass-frames.html

The Year in Kickstarter—2014: https://www.kickstarter.com/year/2014

Sony FES Watch: https://www.makuake.com/project/feswatch/

Qrio Smartlock: https://www.makuake.com/project/qrio-smart-lock/

We interviewed Kunitake Saso, a customer insight specialist at Sony, about its experimentation with crowdfunding.

La Petite Syrah: http://www.lapetitesyrah.fr/

Libélula Brechó: http://brecholibelula.blogspot.com/

Vodacom CEO's Twitter use: http://www.businessinsider.com/pieter-uys-twitter-2011-7

Coffee Joulies' post on being "Made in America or Made in China?": https://madmimi.com/p/da8353

CULTURE

[6.1] Your Trend Department

On the power of 3D objects, Jody Culham studied the limits of visual representations (pictures) to trigger people's imagination, discovering that they are less stimulating than if the same objects would be put in people's hands http://www.ncbi.nlm.nih.gov/pmc/articles/PMC3216611/

KILN personal interview

Malcolm Devoy, one of the creative forces behind PHD Source, told us more abut the platform's effectiveness. More on how this tool works: http://blog.codeworldwide.com/?p=1346#sthash.jWWqvz4b.dpbs

Rajiv Ball from THNK told us in detail about the project in an interview. THNK's press release about the program: http://www.thnk.org/2012/01/vodafone-participates-in-creative-leadership-program/

We had the pleasure to speak about Strategyzer & Master Card with Alexander Osterwalder while he was visiting London to launch his new book, *Value Proposition Design*.

We had a great chat over Skype with Maria Mujica, regional marketing director—Leader, Fly Garage at Mondelez.

More about how Fly Garage inspires innovation in Latin America: http://adage.com/article/global-news/krafts-fly-garage-inspires-innovation-latin-america/235283/

We watched Mark Randall launch Adobe's innovation program Red Box at a keynote at Seoul Digital Forum 2014: https://www.youtube.com/watch?v=2YcbcMRVDQU#t=781

Now, the Red Box is open source: https://kickbox.adobe.com/kickbox-at-your-organization

Richard Wilkinson, Customer Cup innovation manager, shared insights about the project in an interview with us. Aviva's annual report confirms the success of the project: http://www.aviva.com/media/upload/ARA-2013.pdf

Walmart Labs pioneers digital innovation: http://www.adweek.com/news/technology/473-billion-retailer-wants-be-next-ad-tech-star-161471. Here's a video about how Savings Catcher works: https://www.youtube.com/watch?v=ncHxBW0JpuE. About Westfield's labs: http://www.businesswire.com/news/home/20140528005476/en/Westfield-Labs-Launches-Dine-Time-Food-Experience#.VSjZEJTLfis

[6.2] Trend-Driven Ecosystems

Bill Joy, quoted in: http://www.forbes.com/forbes/2007/1126/031.html

Find out more about our spotter network at: spotters.trendwatching.com

Jeremiah Owyang, founder of Crowd Companies, shared details in an interview with us. You'll find them at http://crowdcompanies.com/

Open Innovation: The New Imperative for Creating and Profiting from Technology by Henry William Chesbrough. You'll find Haas School of Business's study at: https://shop.iao .fraunhofer.de/publikationen/managing-open-innovation-in-large-firms.html

Unilever partners with eYeka: http://www.unilever.com/ mediacentre/pressreleases/2013/ crowdsourcingbidfortorrentoffreshideas .aspx
More stories can be found at: https:// en.eyeka.com/stories/product-development

The first coworking space announcement: http://codinginparadise .org/weblog/2005/08/coworking-community-for-developers-who.html,
Coworking spaces growth: http://www .innovationiseverywhere.com/future-coworking-coworking-visas-corporate-partnerships-real-estate-specialists/

http://www.newsroom.barclays .com/releases/ReleaseDetailPage .aspx?releaseId=3076
GE global Garage tour: http://www .gegarages.com/global-tour/

http://www.economist.com/news/ finance-and-economics/21633883-fear-being-displaced-startups-turning-firms-venture-capitalists-if

We had an interview with Augustin Moro and Ana Segurado, who oversee the Wayra program.
For the latest program data: http:// wayra.co/dashboard

Closing Thoughts

Apple App Store data: https:// www.apple.com/uk/pr/ library/2015/01/08App-Store-Rings-in-2015-with-New-Records .html, https://www.apple.com/uk/pr/ library/2014/01/07App-Store-Sales-Top-10-Billion-in-2013.html
YouTube data: https://www.youtube .com/yt/press/statistics.html
Amazon stock figures: http://export-x .com/2014/08/14/many-products-amazon-sell-2/

Facebook acquisition history: http:// newsroom.fb.com/company-info/

Xiaomi valuation: http://www.wsj.com/ articles/xiaomi-becomes-worlds-most-valuable-tech-startup-1419843430
Uber ride data: http://blog.uber.com/ safety
CircleUp company data: https:// circleup.com/data/

IMAGE CREDITS

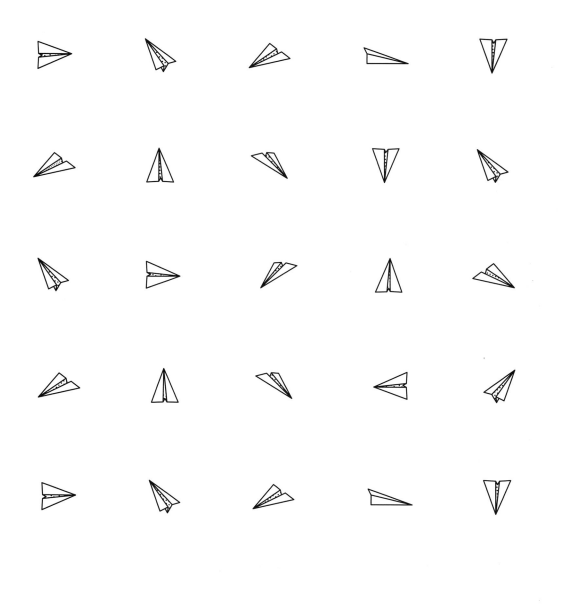

ACKNOWLEDGMENTS

While there are four names listed on the cover of this book, even that dramatically underplays the collective nature of its contents. Countless readers, clients, spotters, colleagues, and friends contributed to this book—knowingly and unknowingly, directly and indirectly—during both the recent months of focused writing and during the years of its longer gestation. A number of people deserve extra thanks, however:

First, the four authors are particularly indebted to Maria Isabel Reyes, who conceived and designed the quite brilliant layout. The quality, comprehension, and impact gap between our original Word documents and the final product is so great that it is nothing but convention keeping her name off the cover of this book. Our words and her design are, at the very least, equal contributors.

Next to Richard Narramore at Wiley, with whom we hatched this book on a summer's afternoon in Central Park, and to our ever-attentive editors Tiffany Colón and Christine Moore. Without your comments this book would have been significantly less well-structured and polished. Also to Lisa di Mona, our agent, who guided us through the world of offline publishing with the utmost care and attention.

Many people kindly gave up their time to speak to us and provided feedback on the drafts of the book, including: James Bidwell, Veronika Bassi, Jean Pierre Beleen, Malcolm Devoy, Sarah Dickinson, Kate Hammer, Nikolai Khlopov, Tom La Forge, Eimear Meredith Jones, Tim Morgan, Augustin Moro, Maria Mujica, Indy Neogy, Rachell Ornan, Alexander Osterwalder, Jeremiah Owyang, Philip Petersen, Jonathan Petrides, BV Pradeep, Jaspar Roos,

Olivier Robert-Murphy, Kunitake Saso, Ana Segurado, Jose Miguel Sokoloff, Jody Turner, Cynthia Vandewall, Grietje Vermoortele, Bas Verhart, Richard Wilkinson, and Michell Zappa. A special mention here should go to Lisa Gansky and Jeffrey Hollender, who were especially generous when sharing their experiences gained during their lifetimes ahead of the trends.

To our TrendWatching colleagues—many of whom are authors in all but name having lived, breathed, and developed this methodology alongside us—thank you for being so patient with us and keeping the business on track while we've had our hands full. Vicki Loomes, Victoria Foster, and Daniel Barcza deserve extra credit for their many helpful contributions.

Our eternal thanks must also go to Reinier Evers, TrendWatching's founder, and still our most perceptive yet demanding trend spotter. He should also be recognized as perhaps the first (and certainly the most frequent) user of the emoticon in business publications, over a decade before it became common practice. :) Thank you for trusting and believing in us all.

Most of all, we would like to thank all our loved ones for their unstinting support. We didn't make things easy with a ludicrously ambitious deadline—through the Christmas "break," an intercontinental relocation, two marriage preparations, and a newborn baby, all coordinated across three time zones. Anita, Baz, Louise, Markus, Meridith (and now Elodie!), we couldn't have done it without you, nor would we want to.

Henry, David, Max, Delia, Maria

OUR TEAM

AUTHORS

HENRY MASON

DAVID MATTIN

MAXWELL LUTHY

DELIA DUMITRESCU

DESIGN

MARIA ISABEL REYES

DANIEL BARCZA

CONTENT

VICTORIA LOOMES

VICTORIA FOSTER

LUCIANA STEIN

REBECA DE MORAES

ACACIA LEROY

LOLA PEDRO

TW:IN (our trend spotter network)

HENRY MASON

Henry runs TrendWatching's global activities on a daily basis and is a sought-after keynote speaker. In the past three years, he has given over 50 keynote presentations in more than 25 countries across six continents. He is regularly quoted as a trend expert, including in the *Financial Times, The New York Times, Fast Company,* and *The Economist*; as well as appearing on television networks such as CNBC, the BBC, and Al Jazeera. In a past life he was a qualified accountant and is responsible for introducing "flawsome" into the business lexicon.

MAXWELL LUTHY

Maxwell Luthy runs our North American business, regularly delivering keynotes and workshops. Maxwell has also been quoted as a trend expert in the *Financial Times*, The Next Web, and more. Besides spotting trends himself, Maxwell also oversaw TW:IN, the company's trend spotter network until 2013, hosting meetups everywhere from Johannesburg to Manila. He now lives in the future trend hot spot of New Jersey, where he *knows* it's only a matter of time until he is discovered for his unique singing voice and lyrical flair.

DAVID MATTIN

David Mattin is our Global Head of Trends & Insights. Across a 12-year career spent thinking about technological, social, and cultural change, David has been a journalist at *The Times*, presented documentaries for the BBC, and appeared in a wide range of international publications, from *The National* to *Google Think Quarterly*. Today, David is a court jester to twin toddler sons Jacob and Leo, a columnist for *BA Business Life*, and an accomplished keynote speaker, appearing regularly at conferences and brand events.

DELIA DUMITRESCU

Delia Dumitrescu is our Lead Innovation Architect, developing and delivering workshops that help participants throughout Europe and the Middle East become innovation-ready. Born in Romania, she lived in Perugia, Barcelona, and Berlin until she decided to put down roots in the world's most livable city, Vienna. This is Delia's fourth book since she wrote *Road Trip to Innovation—How I Came to Understand Future Thinking* in 2012. She was featured in *Forbes Romania's* Top 30 Under 30 in 2014.

INDEX

Index

. . . .

Index

....

Index

. . . .

Index

. . . .